FAITH. FAMILY.
FULFILLMENT.

FAITH. FAMILY. FULFILLMENT.

THROUGH THE SAME LENS
EMBRACING OUR SHARED LIFE VISION

CHRIS & SUZANNE VESTER

BMD
PUBLISHING

BMD Publishing
A division of Market Domination LLC

www.MarketDominationLLC.com
BMDPublishing@MarketDominationLLC.com

Copyright © 2024 Chris and Suzanne Vester
FAITH. FAMILY. FULFILLMENT
Through the Same Lens: Embracing Our Shared Life Vision

All rights reserved.

Sale of this book without a front cover may be unauthorized. If this book is coverless, it may have been reported to the publisher as "unsold or destroyed" and neither the author nor the publisher has received payment for it.

No part of this publication may be reproduced, stored in a retrieval system, or transmitted in any form or by any means, electronic, mechanical, photocopying, recording, or otherwise, without the prior written permission of the Publisher. Requests to the Publisher for permission should be sent to BMD Publishing, 5888 Main Street, Suite 200, Williamsville, NY 14221.

Printed in the United States of America
ISBN # 979-8324979133

BMD PUBLISHING CEO - SETH GREENE
EDITORIAL MANAGEMENT BY BRUCE CORRIS
BOOK DESIGN & LAYOUT BY KRISTIN WILLIAMS

TABLE OF CONTENTS

Dedication vii
Acknowledgments ix

Why Us? Why This Book? 1

1. Dream Mastery 11
2. Managing Your Mindset 19
3. What We Wish We Knew Before Saying "I Do" 29
4. Yes, You Should Sweat the Small Stuff 44
5. Parenting with God in Mind 53
6. Grounded in Gratitude 64
7. Purpose in the Pain 74
8. Defining Success 85
9. Conflicts are Essential 95
10. Processes & Respond Versus Act 107
11. The Wisdom of Words 119
12. What the World Needs Now 131

What's Next? 145

DEDICATION

This book is dedicated to You…

You, the person who is searching for vision and purpose in life

You, the person who desires to leave a legacy

You, the person who wants to love more

You, the person who needs an encouraging word

You, the person who is struggling through hard things

You, the person who just got good news

You, the person who feels overwhelmed

You, the person who is praying for a miracle

You, the person who is searching for HOPE

You, the person who God loves so much

You, the person that was meant to be right here, right now, reading this book

You, this book is dedicated to you

ACKNOWLEDGMENTS

To grow and become your best, you must have family and tribe. They keep you grounded, humble, and driven towards excellence. We have amazing families and a remarkable chosen tribe. We have learned the value of resilience, the joy of hard work, the importance of treating everyone with kindness and respect, and most importantly, putting God first in everything we do. For all of that, we thank you!

Avery, Gabrielle, and Shelby, your presence enriches our lives more than you know. Thank you for the wisdom you've both imparted and inspired. As you embark on your journey, remember that you hold the power to change the world, starting where your feet are.

We want to thank Bailey Whitley Photography (@baileywhitleyphoto) for our cover image, you are the best at capturing the essence of those you photograph, and Bruce Corris and Kristin Williams for their patience and expertise. Bruce, we especially appreciate you and your dedication to this project.

WHY US? WHY THIS BOOK?

If you've listened to our podcast or read our first book, you already know our story…or at least part of it. If so, bear with us while we share it with those of you who are new to us. But even if you are familiar with us, there have been some significant changes we'd like to share with you.

Either way, we think it's important to begin this book by letting you know a little bit about us…our past, our present, and maybe our future. All of which will set the stage for what you'll see in the coming pages. We hope that by understanding who we are and how we got to this point, you'll get more out of the thoughts and insights we'll be sharing, and have a better sense of how to apply them in your own lives.

We're thankful that we've been able to learn a lot of valuable lessons in our lives. Lessons that have helped us have a stronger relationship with each other, with our kids, and with our faith. If sharing them with you helps you do the same, we'll be even more grateful.

Let's start with our backstory.

SUZANNE'S STORY

Suzanne grew up in Mount Pleasant, North Carolina, a small town near Charlotte. Very small…just two stoplights back then and only 132 kids in her high school graduating class. But growing up there was a wonderful experience. Her family was very close. She lived near both her grandparents and her great-grandparents.

She graduated from North Carolina State with a degree in psychology and worked in that field for a bit, but had always been very interested in wellness and health and physical fitness, so she shifted gears and got a master's degree in applied nutrition. Since our first book, she has finished work on her PhD (more on that in a bit), so we're now Doctor and Mister Vester!

CHRIS' STORY

Chris grew up in Nashville, North Carolina, a slightly bigger small town (three stoplights) but a much larger high school, with a graduating class of 365. His family was also very close. His grandparents lived next door.

His dad was a farmer, then switched to insurance sales, and eventually built a successful auto business, owning multiple dealerships. Chris started working there at 17, washing cars, and worked his way up to running the company. He also went to North Carolina State, which is where we met. He graduated with a business degree.

GROWING OUR FAMILY

We've now been together 30 years, married for 27, and have three daughters, ages 23, 19, and 14.

In some ways, having that family is a bit of a miracle. We had a significant health crisis early in our marriage. Just before our second anniversary, Chris was diagnosed with testicular cancer. Imagine beginning to think about having a family and being told, "You can't do that now, and you may never be able to do that." But we both felt Chris was going to be okay. We had faith. As it turned out, we learned we were pregnant with the oldest two years to the day after we received that cancer diagnosis. Chris likes to say that was God's way of saying, "I've got you."

THE ROLE OF FAITH

That is just one example of how important faith is in our lives. For both of us, it started when we were very young. For example, Chris was born on Super Bowl Sunday, 1972, and he was in church with his parents the next Sunday. We both were raised in families with a strong commitment to faith, and as we've moved through adulthood, it has become a stronger pillar in our lives.

It has helped us through some tough times in our marriage. Life isn't always kind. You need something far bigger than yourself to deal with everything that gets thrown at you. Faith has become that very critical and very intentional aspect of our lives.

One of the worst times in our life happened when we bought a business from someone we knew and trusted, but who misled us and sold us a bill of goods. That caused us a tremendous amount of financial strain, which led to disagreements and bitterness and resentment, and a ripple effect that touched just about every aspect of our lives. But we survived, with help from faith-based counseling that drastically shifted how we saw our marriage and saw life in general. It wasn't the end of our struggles, but it led us to a way to overcome them. To this day, whenever we have struggles of any kind, we look back to those sessions and think about what we learned.

WORK-LIFE BALANCE

There's a good reason this will be discussed in this book. Chris works in a field with a very high divorce rate. People work long hours, and many never learn how to overcome that and have the work-life balance that's critical to any marriage.

In our case, while Suzanne was home with the kids much more than Chris, she learned something many couples don't learn, which is the importance of understanding the reason your spouse is doing what they do. It's not because they don't want to be with you or the kids. In most cases, they're doing it out of a sense of duty. And there are ways to make the best of it.

When Chris worked six days a week, we still had Sundays. If he worked nights, we made the most of the evenings when he was home for a family dinner. We still had date night, and we took vacations. It took planning, but if you're not intentional about this, it's not going to happen. And when it doesn't happen, that's when you start feeling disconnected from each other.

Suzanne has coached people on this. The scales aren't always balanced in life. But is there harmony? Look at the solar system. Sometimes the earth is closer to the sun, and sometimes it's further away, but we're never going to fall off the planet because we're always in harmony.

When you see that it's about harmony, not balance, you can live a more integrated life. For us, faith is like the sun of our solar system.

WHAT'S NEW WITH US?

While we've both seen some changes since our first book came out, Suzanne's have been much more dramatic. First, as we mentioned earlier, she completed her doctorate and now has a PhD in Biblical Naturopathy. But what she's doing with that degree is much different than her original plans. She made a very significant decision that instead of having a for-profit business, she would have a non-profit ministry, and focus on women and families. This changes how she can serve people. There's more flexibility to provide the services most needed and there's more opportunity to help in meaningful ways.

Suzanne has always said she would do what she does for free if she could. But the rent has to be paid, and the lights need to stay on…and of course having some income is a good thing.

But it's always been in her mind to find a way to do this so anyone can be served. Doing it as a nonprofit means we can raise money, we can do scholarships, we can have a process for benevolence. If somebody needs a service but just cannot afford it, they'll have a way to be served.

Sometimes, serving people doesn't necessarily mean you're going to solve anything for them. You're just giving them permission and space and support so they can begin to move down that process on their own. There was a way to do that in the original business model, but unless someone could afford the initial consultation Suzanne couldn't really help them, because how could she justify that to the people who are paying for it?

Chris is still in the same position at the business, but he's doing more work outside the business. He's working with other entrepreneurs, helping them to grow their businesses. The neat thing is, these are not necessarily businesses that are directly involved with him. But business struggles are often universal to many industries, so he's able to help. He's not getting paid for this, but he's getting satisfaction seeing others grow the way his business has.

Meanwhile, at his business, he's more future-focused. They want to do more things that are ministry-driven and events-driven. As a family business, how will that look inside and outside the family? How will the business evolve? The family is now getting together on a regular basis to discuss this. That's the two of us, Chris' sister and her husband, and his parents. They're looking at ways the business could underwrite something that could pour into the community in a way that would give back, especially when it comes to families. It's pretty exciting.

That's not the only way the two of us can collaborate on the business. We're getting the chance to work together more often because Suzanne is serving as a performance coach. We'll talk more about that in an upcoming chapter, because there's a lot there to unpack. We should point out; this was a request from the leadership team. Chris had struggled with the idea of doing this because it certainly had the appearance of nepotism. But the reaction has only been positive, and it's having a big impact on both the business and the people.

On the family front, our older daughters are at the age where they're involved with young men, in some cases fairly seriously, and their relationships are new relationships for us as well. We're enjoying this stage of parenthood. Chris in particular is building a nice rapport with them, and appreciates the fact that they're able to reach out to him when they have questions or struggles. They don't just tolerate the old man; they seem to enjoy being in his company. We're pretty sure he'll be walking someone down the aisle in the next few years.

Chris has also been asked to be a big part of the men's ministry at our church. He's teaching a curriculum that he brought in, leading men through how to develop to lead their families, and lead in their businesses, and just lead themselves well. This came to him on a mission trip in South Asia, where he was asked to lead men on an initiative that was actually the same type of coaching that he'd been doing at work. Life works out in funny ways sometimes.

THE NEXT STEPS:

Even though this book leans heavily toward couples and families, that doesn't mean you shouldn't read it if you're not married or in a serious relationship. When Chris talks to young men who aren't married or not even dating, one of his challenges to them is, "If you want to be a great husband, start being one before there's even a woman in your life." We've all fallen into the category of someone who struggles and doubts their next step. If you've ever asked yourself whether you're doing the right thing, this book won't answer that question for you but it will certainly initiate a lot of thoughts and conversations.

That's really how we see this book, as a conversation starter. As Suzanne referenced earlier when talking about her practice, sometimes what's needed is support more than a solution. There are plenty of marriage therapy books that profess to solve the issues you're facing. You can't get that from a book. But you can get the impetus to talk not just about the challenges you're facing, but also the things that are going well.

People often tell Suzanne she has a big toolbox. Think of this book that way. It's not, "You have questions, we have answers." It's more like, "If you have questions, we have tools to help you get your answers, and ask better questions."

So start asking.

1

DREAM MASTERY

Being from North Carolina, we know that the "Dream Team" was Michael Jordan and his teammates on the 1992 Olympic basketball team. But did you know that you have your own Dream Team? And it plays a significant role in your marriage.

This dream team consists of you, your spouse, and God. It allows us to put our dreams into written form and plan them out, making sure they align with God and that we do our part to make our spouse's dreams come true. Doing that is actually the job description of a biblical spouse.

Dream teaming is sitting down and affirming everything you've done up to this point and making sure everyone is on board with all of it. Look at what's being planned out. Does it align with both your spouse and with God? Do you understand what it's going to require of you, and are you okay with it? If so, then you can move forward, because you need to both be pursuing the same thing, and you both need to be on the same page.

Think of it as an accountability checkup. "Hey, we're in this together. We've come to the conclusion this is where we're headed as a family, as a couple, and as individuals, involving our marriage, our family, our careers, calling and purpose." All of that has become really clear.

We often sit with people and ask them, "What does it look like for you 10 years from now?" They seldom have an answer. That can be due to a lack of exposure to the idea, or the lack of permission to dream beyond what they know. It's hard to do that on your own. Sometimes you need a push.

As Chris and his dad have gone through the process of building their business, they've developed a sense of intuition. But if you've never been in that situation, the idea of going to the next step is something that's foreign to you. That's the lack of exposure. Or, if you never feel like you're worthy of going after what you feel God has put on your heart because of your environment or the mindset you grew up around, that's the permission aspect. You're thinking, "Hey, nobody ever told me that this was okay."

We believe that goes back to not limiting the ability of God because God is infinitely powerful, infinitely great, and can put those puzzle pieces together in ways that we cannot even imagine. Knowing and acknowledging that, and then limiting yourself, is saying that you don't believe in that. So, you have to be very careful to not let your own experiences and thoughts get in your way. Especially being able to let go of the belief that if you're being tasked with doing something you don't feel qualified for, you won't even try to do it, or you'll go in with the belief that you can't do it, which means you'll fail.

It's important to remember God's role as the third member of our Dream Team. He will help us accomplish this. Knowing that, and knowing he's part of the team, will significantly help us move forward with success. You're not on your own. A big takeaway for a lot of people is acknowledging, "I came to the end of myself and then this happened." That's okay. Just understand, you don't have to see it through to the conclusion. No one is asking you to do it in your own power.

That's a new way of thinking for many people. It won't be in your power, but it's still going to come to fruition. Often, we think we can do it all. But then we ask, "If I can do it all, why haven't I?"

When we really focus on it, we realize that we've been through this process collectively. Including God as the third member of the Dream Team creates this environment of alignment between you, your spouse, and God...and He's the leading factor.

There's certainly some theology involved in this. Some understanding of God's word. Understanding that leads to other alignments coming into your space and your life, very strategically. At some point, you are going to need those alignments to move forward.

In our case, we've given ourselves permission to explore the things that were on our heart. Like our podcast, and this book. Just saying yes when prodded, and continuing to do that, has led us to expand our thinking on what we can be a part of. It's exposed us to people who are going to come alongside us because they know that in their situation, we're going to come alongside them with their needs.

It's knowing that there are going to be alignments that will further accelerate the process of that dream coming to fruition.

It's also going to keep you from getting stuck. It's going to keep you moving forward.

The easiest place for someone to get stuck is really just getting started. We rarely stop and imagine potential possibilities. Instead, we get too burdened down by the grind of the day and our responsibilities. It's difficult to carve out that space where you can just explore and dream, and understand that it might not be a tomorrow dream. It might be a 10-year dream. Just having the space and permission can make a huge difference.

Many people don't know they have permission to think about this. We do have permission to step into that possibility. If you can't do that, if you've never thought about the dream storming part of it, it can be overwhelming. You think about what you have, not what you can be. Our tendency is to go into that space of requirements and responsibilities, and all these things that tangentially are part of the equation. When we get down to the brass tacks of planning it out, putting it into place, we have to consider those things.

But it's not part of the dreaming part, and it's so hard for us to remove that part. Because we deal with it every day. We have limited time. We have limited resources. If you own a business, you're always coming up against bumpers. So that dream casting component of it could be really hard for folks because they've never really thought outside of their day-to-day restrictions.

On the other hand, we're told we can be anything we want as long as we're willing to put in the work and the sacrifice. We've all said that to our kids. We've all asked them what they're willing to sacrifice. So, the storming part of it really needs to be revisited, and revisited, and revisited some more until we say, "Okay, I can't think any bigger with my mind." Now you're ready." You could spend days and days storming until you reach the point where you're dreaming so big you can't even imagine where it's going. If not, you're going to shortchange yourself.

Then, when you are ready, it's all about making that big impact. We talk about this a lot with our kids. Our children truly want to solve world problems. When they see a problem, they want to do something about it. Even if they think their piece of it will be small, that doesn't stop them from trying. They don't discount themselves or their lack of impact. They believe, "Even if it's just a tiny part, I'm still a part of it." We're very proud of them for that.

So, how do you go about this? If you look at something and think, "Well, that's probably achievable for almost anybody," then go one bigger than that. And keep going bigger. Because if anyone can do it, how is it special to you? This is a daunting task, but the great thing about it is once there's a plan in place and it's on paper, you know you're linking together. You're linking arm in arm to achieve each other's dreams. Your dream is my dream and my dream is your dream. Helping your spouse fulfill their dreams is a huge purpose for you.

But here's a word of caution. Those who love you the most want to protect you. So, if you're sharing big dreams with people who don't share that same ability to look at things they can't see, feel or touch, don't let them discount your dream. Don't let them discourage you, or talk you out of something you've decided on because they love you and want to protect you. Sometimes that love and protection have a really high price tag, and that is keeping you from achieving what you have been put on this planet to achieve.

We want to recommend a book that will help you with this process, so it makes more sense. It's called *The Dream Giver* by Bruce Wilkinson. It's easy to read, or listen to on Audible because it's not a study book or a textbook, it's a story book. It's literally listening to a story played out about someone who has a dream on their heart. It follows the stages of the process they go through, including having conversations with their loved ones, and being told, "I don't think that's a safe idea." It explains why it makes sense that someone would say that, and why it makes sense that sometimes you shouldn't listen.

But in the end, those who know us best and love us most are going to understand that anyone who is going through this is not doing it simply out of their own personal want, will and desire. They understand the bigger picture, that it's about Kingdom work. They understand that this was not a quick impulsive decision. Ideally, they won't try to discourage the dreaming and the doing because they know it's coming from a place that is grounded and is going to bear fruit.

TAKEAWAYS FROM THIS CHAPTER

God can help you plan out your dreams, but you have to let him onto your "Dream Team". That means not letting your limiting beliefs get in the way. It means making sure your plans align with your spouse and with God, and you understand what's required of you.

- If you alone can do it all, why haven't you?
- What does it look like to "Come to the end of yourself?"
- What is your BHAG (big hairy audacious goal)?

2

MANAGING YOUR MINDSET

We're all going to face challenging circumstances in our lives from time to time. How you handle them is key. You can either say "Woe is me," or you can use them as a learning experience. That means shifting your mindset from "it's happening to me" to "it's happening *for* me."

This came up for us recently when we were traveling internationally. One of our flights was cancelled on our trip home, giving us a "wonderful" overnight stay in Jamaica, Queens, New York. Chris was able to use that time to finally get his global entry interview done, so Suzanne no longer needs to stand in a customs line with him.

It's all about changing your perspective on how you handle disappointments, or for that matter, everyday situations. It's changing your language from "I have to do this" to "I get to do this." Rather than feeling you have to go to work, you get to go to work, and you have the opportunity to be impactful in ways that are only for you.

Not to mention, there are plenty of people who would change places with you in any given situation, because their situation is worse. How arrogant is it to assume that your issues and your problems are worse than everyone else's?

We learned this lesson early in our relationship. It was about six weeks before our wedding. We lived in Shelby, North Carolina, a great little city. Chris was working for his dad and Suzanne was in graduate school. We had it all planned, we were going to be a big part of the community. Suzanne had already moved into the house we were going to live in.

But then, things changed. Business issues resulted in Chris being moved to the business in Clinton, five hours away. Talk about a disruption! Six weeks before our wedding our lives were turned upside down, including not knowing where we would live. We ended up moving in with Chris's parents for a while.

Needless to say, there was a lot of frustration. There were a lot of tears, and Suzanne is not a crier. It would have been easy to just bemoan what happened. But instead, we look back on that as an early example of the resiliency of our relationship.

It changed our trajectory. There were only two schools in the state that offered the program Suzanne was in, and neither was anywhere near where we were going to live. And forget the job offers she already had in Shelby. This derailed her career plans.

The one thing it didn't change was our wedding. We kind of plowed through it, and proceeded with our plans, and had the wedding we had always wanted. But we never sat down and had a real conversation about what would be next. That was the great unknown.

But we soldiered on. And if that hadn't happened, Suzanne wouldn't have ended up where she is now professionally, which is where she was absolutely meant to be, and which lets her help people in ways that would never have been possible before. And our kids wouldn't have grown up near their grandparents and great-grandparents. Not a lot of people have the opportunity to do that.

Yes, at the time it was a disappointment and a frustration, but we can say, "Okay, it led to this, which led to this, and so on." It's all connected.

We all know that hindsight is 20/20. The point of all this is to not wait to look back with hindsight, but react in the moment. Reevaluate, and say, "Okay, what's the positive here? How is this a benefit to me?" Even though it may hurt at that moment, or be uncomfortable, or be off plan, what does the other side of this look like for you?

Chris went through this with the business in 2020 when Covid hit and it seemed the world had lost its mind. He had a conversation with all the dealerships and told them it was his responsibility to come up with the vision of what things would look like. He was brutally honest, and told them he had no idea how they were going to come out of this. But he also said, "I can promise you that we're going to come out better than we went in. We're going to double down on customer service. We're going to get better with knowledge. We're going to educate ourselves on what the customer is looking for in a better way, so when things go back to normal, we're able to serve them better."

Although it didn't happen to the degree he wanted, the business is light years ahead of where it was pre-Covid in how they're dealing with customers, and the culture of the business, and the direction it's headed.

You might be thinking, "We don't own a business. What does this have to do with our marriage?" Consider this: one of the things that helped the business deal with this was they had a vision. It was actually written down. "This is where we are, this is where we're headed, and this is where we want to be." Having a business plan is crucial if you want to have a successful business.

But you can also do that with your family. When we got married, and began having children, we had a vision of what we thought our family life was going to look like, but not nearly to the degree we do now, because we were much less intentional then. We hadn't learned the importance of actually creating a family plan and writing it down. That way, if things change and you end up on a different path, you can say, "Wait a minute. This doesn't meet our vision. How can we still get there?"

There will always be bumps in the road. But having it written down allows you to lean back on something that's concrete and well thought-out and say, "Okay, where's the side road? Where's the back road navigation? How do we find a different way to get there?" The beauty lies in what you're learning in the back room.

It's not easy. Our oldest daughter doesn't adapt well to things not working out as she planned. She's been that way since she was young. One time she planned a sleepover, and it was totally planned out. She was disappointed when everybody left because they didn't get to do all the things she had planned. Suzanne asked her, "But did you have fun?" She said, "Yes, we had a great time." So, why did it matter to her? That's just her nature.

When we've drawn a picture in our mind of what we think something should look like, and when we get there and it doesn't look that way, we have two choices. We can embrace where we are, celebrate the victories that got us there, reassess and move on, or we can get angry that it didn't turn out exactly as we had planned, pout about it and not take away anything from it.

It's really important to be able to look at where you are and celebrate the wins, or reassess if you need to, in order to move forward. Don't get hung up in what didn't turn out as you hoped or envisioned, because there's always room for adjustment. You have to be resilient, and you have to have a certain amount of perseverance, to just keep moving and not get stuck.

Jesse Itzler said something pertinent to this. He said if he looks at the common denominator among people who are successful, it's grit. Being able to recognize that sometimes you have to bear down and get through it. Not folding to the disappointment, not folding to the distraction, not folding to the disruption. Just having the grit and fortitude to power through. To re-plan, readjust, reassess and recalculate, which sometimes may mean a revision of your vision.

On our podcast, we talked about vision casting. Part of that was staging. But when something throws us for a loop or disrupts our vision, many times the only thing it changes is the stage itself. If you have a plan, and you have it written down, you can recognize, "All I need to do is move the staging. Because I had this much done. Okay, this happened. What's the setback? What am I learning? What can be adjusted and reevaluated? And what does it do to the ultimate vision?" In most cases, it actually makes it better.

The next step is to re-stage it. When is it going to happen? In the next two years? Maybe four? If not then, can it happen in the next 10 years? In managing the frustrations and the disappointments, you have to look at it in the future. You have to ask, "Okay, in five years, is this situation really going to make a difference? What about in 10 years?" If the answer to either question is no, then just move through it, because it's not going to change, or not change so much that you're going to feel it down the road.

That's because the vision is going to be what it should be. Where you're going is still where you're going. Just remember, success is never linear, and neither is life.

So, get it down on paper. Collaborate over it with your spouse. Come together, so when those rogue waves of the world bump you, you can say, "It's not happening to us. It's happening for us." And try to assess the benefit of it happening the way it is versus the way you planned.

When you're looking at it from that vantage point, it's also important to remember this. God typically has three answers to your request and prayers. It's either yes, no, or not yet, I have something better. If you feel the answer is no, don't be frustrated and angry. Just know that there's something else on the horizon. Don't get stuck where you are and miss out on what's coming.

And don't quit. When people get where they want to be, they say, "Well, I finally succeeded." They succeeded because they kept going. They tried one more time. They tried one more thing. Don't sell yourself short and quit before you have that breakthrough or that success.

Things are always going to get off track in family life. There will also be things that come along that can rock your faith. But if we keep our mind on the fact that there is a sovereign plan, and His ways are better than our ways, and are in alignment with Christ, it won't keep you from having struggles, but in those situations, you'll know it's okay because you still have an anchor. You're not going to be adrift. You're still tethered, you're still anchored, and that makes it easier to go through those moments of frustration or setback or just the unknown.

TAKEAWAYS FROM THIS CHAPTER

You've heard the saying "mind over matter". We think a better choice is "Your mindset matters." What you think goes a long way toward determining how you feel.

- Think about what has happened FOR you recently.
- What is your vision?
- How do you celebrate wins?
- Can you think of a yes, no or not yet from God in your life?
- Don't Quit!

3

WHAT WE WISH WE KNEW BEFORE SAYING "I DO"

People say it all the time: "I wish I had known that back then." We might have done things differently, or made better decisions. While it's easy to look back with the benefit of hindsight, what's done is done. We all learned a lot as we went along.

But it's a good exercise for any couple to each come up with a list of five things they wish they knew as they entered their marriage, and then compare that list. You might be surprised how many things you both came up with.

Here's our list. There's more than five, because each of us came up with our own list, but there was actually some overlap between us, and we both agree on everything here. You'll also see that some of them have a strong connection to others.

GET PLUGGED INTO A COMMUNITY OF BELIEVERS AND THEN SERVE

Everyone is selfish to some extent. But when you're in service, selfishness is less likely to crop up because you're not focusing on yourself, you're focusing on outside.

Who's in your circle? When we've intentionally looked for who's in our circle and cultivated that, it has served us well. It's also changed our daughters' circle, and even how they think and react to the world and their space.

Our oldest daughter told Chris a story about the Christian camp where she works. That camp has been very impactful for her. As you can imagine, the camp was deeply affected by Covid. For the first time in two years, they were able to let the Department of Juvenile Justice bring kids there. We're not saying these are bad kids, but it's a population she had not been exposed to in her life.

She said, "Daddy, you and Mom always say language is important and that's something we've picked up and we talk about a lot. Language is important." She said she saw that the way those kids got spoken to every day made a difference.

The other thing she learned was the way we think is different than many other families, because of the circles we're in, and we've put our daughters in. Because of the environment we've intentionally put them in. This wasn't always easy for us as parents, but this reinforced the value of doing this.

THERAPY IS A THING

For many couples, marriage counseling or marriage therapy is something you only go to when there's a problem. But many times, if you wait until there's a problem, it's too late.

Given Chris' experience in the auto industry, it's only natural that he makes this analogy: If you treat it like maintenance, it's more effective. Oil changes and tire rotations and things like that protect your car and cost you less in the long run.

The first time we went to therapy it was the result of a large struggle in our marriage. Chris did not want to do it even then. But we went, and we put in a lot of work, and it helped us tremendously. But that didn't mean we were done. For us, this faith-based counseling has kept our tires inflated and made the road much smoother.

Suzanne tells her clients that sometimes you just need to referee to say to one spouse, "Hey, you hush," and tell the other one, "You say what you've got to say," and then do it again in reverse order. It's having someone to enforce that so you don't talk over each other. When you do that, you're not listening. You're not hearing anything.

DEFINE YOUR BOUNDARIES EARLY AND OFTEN

There are a lot of boundaries, particularly early in a marriage, because you're not just marrying your spouse, you're marrying their family. What are their expectations for holidays, birthdays, and so on? What about how they raise their grandchildren? What about gifts and snacks and other treats?

But the truly important boundaries are in your marriage. What are the lines that you and your spouse do not cross? You have to define them early and then refine them as you and your marriage evolve.

What comes to mind most often are the boundaries when it comes to opposite sex relationships, whether that's friends, coworkers or members of your church. Where do you draw the line, and where is it overstepping?

It can be very easy in the workplace to get comfortable with someone of the opposite sex, and things can get out of hand. We often spend more of our waking hours with our coworkers than with our spouse. How many times have you heard someone say, "She's my work wife," or "He's my work husband"? That's really not a healthy term to use.

Your spouse should always be number one. If someone else is feeling as though they have that role or that space and they are overstepping, then it's time to reevaluate.

NEVER SAY "ASK MOM" (OR DAD)

True confession time. We violate this one a lot (Chris more than Suzanne). We should have trained ourselves better. When our three daughters were growing up, they were very good at dividing and conquering. There have been numerous occasions when we weren't on the same page because of miscommunication or a lack of communication between us.

Kids aren't thinking, "Hey, let's drive a wedge between our parents," they just want to get their way. And one of the quickest ways to do that is to separate the parents and get one to say yes and one to say no. If that leads to an argument between the parents, so be it. The child is still expecting things to work out for them.

For many couples, the only conversation about children before they get married is whether they both want to have them. Once they're married, they talk about when kids should come along. Then, once they become parents, they still rarely talk about having that unified front.

But that's something that should be discussed, because biblically speaking, you cleave to your spouse first. This may sound harsh if you haven't been taught the way we've been taught, but the spouse comes first, and then the children, and then the family you left. It's how the hierarchy of family works.

If your children see you as a unified front, it gives them a really good picture of what marriage can be, and what they can strive for in looking for a spouse.

And there's more to it than just yes or no. When one of our daughters comes to Suzanne, she often asks, "Have you asked your father?" Routinely the answer is, "He told me to ask you." There was usually more to the conversation than that, but that's all they heard.

HOW DO YOU RESOLVE CONFLICT?

Every marriage has conflict. Every successful marriage resolves that conflict. But everyone does that differently. What's out of bounds for you? What language is out of bounds? What behavior? Is it okay to walk out and slam a door to let off steam?

Even though we're very aware of this, we still fall back into bad patterns. We still have conversations about what is not acceptable. We still find ourselves in situations where one or both of us have to apologize to the other because of violating what we knew was our standard for who we are as a couple. It's so important to define what's acceptable, and know when it gets out of bounds. More important, how to avoid going beyond what's recoverable.

Sometimes that's as simple as taking a time out. Saying, "We need to go to our corners and revisit this later. We're not going to constructively handle this if we continue." Because when you get emotional, you dig in, and then you go nowhere. You're no longer listening.

DATING DOESN'T STOP

We've talked to many couples on our podcast, and they've often said something that we've taken to heart over the years.

Dating is important. Don't stop dating just because you're married. It can make a big difference in your relationship.

We became very intentional about this fairly early in our marriage, when our oldest daughter was around two years old. We would get Chris' parents to keep her overnight. That let us do not just date night, but an overnight date. We would go and stay somewhere, just to get away. At that time, we both had full-time jobs and a business, and the baby. These dates weren't about romance, they were about spending time together, just the two of us.

Unfortunately, we got away from that for a while. Chris was traveling a lot with his job, and affordability became an issue. But dates don't have to be expensive. You don't need a hotel room and a costly dinner; you just need to be with each other. As we look back, we think if we had stayed focused on this, we might not have had some of the struggles we faced, or at least they would have been less severe.

Several of our podcast guests have told us that if they miss a date, they don't connect as well. Issues start to arise. They start to see chinks in each other. We've heard ourselves in those comments. When you're not dating your spouse, you don't have that time you need to sit down and evaluate the family, evaluate yourselves and where you're headed.

You intentionally date each other before marriage. You may have fallen in love on a date. So why not keep it going? We've seen in our marriage that when we're very intentional about our dating, everything around our marriage flourished, even our kids' space, because we discuss them so much.

Don't let being married keep you from dating.

LEARN HOW TO NURTURE AND FEED YOUR SPOUSE'S SPIRIT AND WHAT SETS THEM ON FIRE

We've known each other for three decades. The specifics of what sets us on fire have changed a lot over the years, but in general terms, we're very much still the same.

For example, back in college, if Chris really liked a class, he was all in. If he didn't, he pretty much checked out. Over the years, he's felt that way about many things. When he's all in on something, he jumps in, figures it out, gets it done, and moves on.

For Suzanne, the challenge has been learning how to appreciate that, especially when it's not something that feeds her fire. In effect, it's like learning how to feed something that is completely foreign to you.

But you have to do that. You have to let your spouse do things that set them on fire, even if you don't understand it. You need to learn how to enrich that, whether that's by giving space, giving affirmation, giving encouragement, or providing context, like finding something that fits in with what you want.

For Chris, sometimes this means leaving Suzanne alone. Her fire has changed as she's evolved professionally, to now having her own holistic health practice where she leads people to physical and spiritual well-being in a biblical way. Chris has certainly followed along and paid close attention as she worked toward her doctorate and established her practice, but it's her wheelhouse. Leaving her alone means enjoying it without having to know all the intricate details.

It's easier to feed their spirit when you know how to communicate with them, which leads to the next item on our list.

BE COGNIZANT OF WHAT SPEAKS TO THEM AND THEIR LOVE LANGUAGE

Do you know your love languages? Many couples don't. We didn't really understand this until we had our first stumble in our marriage, when we became disconnected. Our therapist taught us this, and we've never forgotten it. He had us take the love language test.

Basically, there are five love languages: acts of service, words of affirmation, physical touch, gifts, and quality time. Different ones take on a different importance to you at different stages of your life. When you're newlyweds, you're focused totally on each other. When you have a child, things change. If one of you has a major career change, that impacts this.

If your personal love language is gifts or acts of service, you may think doing an act of service for your spouse would speak to them because it speaks to you. But if their number one love language is quality time, that act of service doesn't even get recognized. They don't even see it. It's like you're speaking Spanish and they're speaking French.

It's so important that you and your spouse know each other's language and make a conscious effort to speak to each other in that way. It makes a drastic difference in your connection.

This is also important with your children. Knowing your kids' love language helps you have a better relationship. For example, one of our daughters' number one is quality time and her number two is physical touch. So going for a ride in a car with her and holding her hand would be her best day ever. It would really feed her. Knowing that another daughter's number one is physical touch explains why she's a big hugger and why we make sure she gets lots of hugs from us.

PUT YOUR INSECURITIES ON THE TABLE

We were not each other's first boyfriend or girlfriend. But as you go through your developmental years and those beginning relationships, you learn a lot about what you don't want, and some of those things are pretty serious. So when you find the person you're going to marry, it's important that you throw those cards on the table. If you don't know what they are, you'd better figure it out.

This actually circles back to some of the things we mentioned earlier. For example, if you're very insecure about something and it crosses a boundary, or in a moment of conflict something is hurled at you that directly injures that insecurity, then it's going to make it even worse. But not knowing that you're doing that to somebody compounds the issue. If you don't know that you've hurt or injured your spouse, how can you prevent that? The flip side of that is if you do know that's an insecurity and you still do it, then shame on you.

Throwing your insecurities on the table so you can overcome them, or they're not weaponized against you at some point, should pave the way for a much healthier relationship.

VISIONING YOUR NEXT STEP

It took us more than 25 years of marriage to learn about this one. What does the next step in your life look like? That's a pretty deep conversation. A big reason we're at that spot in our life is because our daughters are moving to the next stage in their lives. One graduated from college, one graduated from high school, and the one still in the house isn't going to be here for long.

Defining your vision starts with dreaming about your spouse and your family. What does your marriage look like? What does your family look like? What does your career look like? It means looking at all those things very intentionally. We wish we had been exposed to this idea early in our marriage, because it's a lot easier to have this conversation when there's just the two of you. In our case, we've gone from two to three to four to five. Starting when your family has grown makes it a bit more complicated, and definitely more difficult.

This doesn't just impact our family life. There are things we probably wouldn't have gotten involved with in business if we had been exposed to this process. Case in point, the gym business we had. We've been very open about what a mistake that turned out to be for us. And that one bad decision had a domino effect. It led to many struggles for us. But it wouldn't have even been on our path if we had this type of vision.

Defining your vision means asking yourself what your best life looks like, and then intentionally taking steps toward that life.

So that's our list. What's yours? It doesn't have to be five things. It can be just a couple or even just one. But just coming up with this list and having this conversation can make a big difference in your marriage…and your life.

TAKEAWAYS FROM THIS CHAPTER

Even the best relationship could benefit from a little hindsight. It's very helpful to think about what you know now and how that might have helped you before you got married, or earlier in your marriage. Sitting down and making a list like that can be a real eye-opener.

- What are your top five things?
- Does our list spark any thoughts for you? Can you relate to it?
- What advice would you give your younger self?
- What does preventative action look like in your marriage?
- How can you communicate your boundaries with confidence?

4

YES, YOU SHOULD SWEAT THE SMALL STUFF

We often hear, "Hey, don't sweat the small stuff." But in any relationship, there's importance in the small details. And not only are we not encouraged to think about those things, just the opposite, everyone focuses on the big stuff. Nobody calls attention to the little things, which can mean the most.

In the previous chapter we talked about taking the love language test. One benefit to that is that it lets you know what the small things are, and define which ones need to be paid attention to on behalf of the other person.

This topic came up for us because of a phone call from our oldest daughter. She told us she received a letter in the mail from the young man she was seeing. They were in a long-distance relationship, and they talked all the time, but he took the time to write her a letter. Obviously, she didn't tell us what was in it, but she said it was something they had talked about, and how much the letter meant to her.

> *Quick aside:* Letter writing is a lost art. All three of our daughters are big letter writers, and they love getting mail, whether it's from relatives who live out of town, or friends, or whoever they exchange letters with. Letters are tangible. You can go back and re-read them. You don't have to scroll back through dozens of messages on your phone. A letter is something you can pull out and read again and recall the emotions you felt when you first received it.

But back to this chapter's topic. Her call led us to talk about how we pay attention to the small details in our relationship. It requires time and effort. But it shows that you care and that you're paying attention. You're being intentional.

So, what small stuff should we sweat? It helps to look at people's behavior patterns. If you're really paying attention to your spouse, you'll likely see things that get done consistently, every single day. For example, Chris has certain routines every morning. He sets out his supplements for the day. He walks the dog every morning. There are repetitive patterns, and because Suzanne is very observant and intentional, she can list every single one. She's very good at paying attention to the small, detailed things, and she's very good at finding small, seemingly insignificant ways to say, "I see you, I hear you, I love you, I appreciate you" in whatever form that takes. It would be different from person to person. Chris, on the other hand, is more of a 30,000-foot view kind of thinker, so when he has one of those small, show up gesture moments, it's really kind of big.

We have kind of a funny success story about this. When we had our first Christmas together as a married couple, Chris bought Suzanne a sewing machine. You're probably thinking, "What's the matter, you couldn't get a vacuum cleaner?" But it was a really good gift. Suzanne loves to sew. Chris knew nothing about it, and in fact still doesn't, but he took the time to learn just enough about something Suzanne really enjoys so he could buy the right present.

Figuring out what your spouse enjoys and then taking the initiative to at least know the basics about something you could care less about may seem like a big gesture, but it starts with a lot of small pieces. In this case, it meant paying attention to the fact that it was something Suzanne enjoyed, that it was important to her, and she was going to find great joy in it in the future. Over the years, she has made a lot of our daughters' clothes, not to mention her own.

One way we are intentional about paying attention to the small things is we honor every month that we are together. We're up to more than 360 months as of now. It's unlikely that we would forget, but it's on our calendar every month just in case.

We think it's something every couple can relate to. It's celebrating the little things. And if you celebrate the littles, then there's always something to celebrate. Think about the momentum a relationship can get if you're constantly in a mode of celebration. Because in between those celebrations there are going to be struggles, and some of them will be massive. That's just a fact of life in any relationship. But maybe, if you take those little wins and celebrate them in a big way, then those struggles get a little bit smaller.

The small things are like the pebbles in a riverbed. They're the foundation of a riverbed, and they're foundational in a relationship because they're things you can build on, and revisit over time. Celebrating the small wins and paying attention to the small things that are meaningful can help make the other person feel, "Okay, I'm important."

So now that we've talked about how this benefits our spouses, what about children? How can parents celebrate the small wins and think about the small things for their children? It can start with focusing on the positive.

This is something many parents can probably relate to. Chris has often tried to help one of our daughters because she struggles with a lot of the same things he's struggled with. But looking back, there are things he could have done better, because the way he tried to help often came across as correcting her, or being on her case, even though it was often him just saying, "Hey, this will help."

If you look back at a situation like that and think, "I could have done it better. I could have paid attention to the small things so the course corrections didn't seem so big," that can help you do better the next time. You can help your child celebrate the small wins, instead of focusing on how those small struggles could end up being big. Pay attention to the wins and focus on the positive.

Sweating the small stuff takes work, and can add to all the sweat that already goes into parenting. We all know parenting is exhausting. When you're in the middle of parenting, especially when your children are young, the exhaustion of the day-to-day can make you less able to pay attention to some of the things your kids may be giving you cues on that are really important to them. It can help to just carve out five minutes to take a break and ask yourself, "What can I do today that will be a good thing for tomorrow?" Or do a recap at the end of the day. "What went well for us today? What could have gone better?" If you can make that a practice, it will give you a lot of clues. It will actually give you reference points to pay attention to in the future and how to honor those small things.

Sometimes you just need to surprise kids from time to time. That doesn't mean shower them with gifts, or give them expensive and elaborate presents. This is something Suzanne is very good at. One of our daughters loves tacos and she loves cactuses. She likes to look at cactuses and she likes to eat tacos. One day, Suzanne was walking through a store and they had cactus taco holders. So of course she bought one. She knew our daughter would love it, which she did.

Suzanne gives thoughtful gifts, not just to our family but to everyone. She always asks herself, "Are they going to like this? Are they going to use it? Will they treasure it? Is it going to be meaningful to them?" When you're looking at little things with your kids, you have to ask those same questions. "Is my gesture, my acknowledgement or recognition, going to be treasured? Is it going to be meaningful? Is it going to be something that they look on fondly?" And the only way we can do that is by having intentional one-on-one time, and conversations where you get to know what makes somebody else tick.

If you know what's important to them because you're having those type of conversations, where you're the one asking questions, it leaves clues as to how to honor them, how to pay attention. What are the small things that mean the most?

Sweating the small stuff can also be a benefit at work, particularly if you have a written record of things. Chris is currently working on the branding of his business and it's all about storytelling. If you have the written word, whether that's in notes or letters or a journal, you have the ability to retell stories and showcase changes you may not have noticed over time. You have a better record of the important parts of who you are and who you came to be, which you don't necessarily know unless you are dialed in to the small things.

As you know, Chris' business is family owned. His father started it, and now Chris and his sister are the second generation of leaders. There are many stories about how the business came to be, and for that matter, how the family evolved to where it is today. Through this process, they've been able to share some little stories that had a huge impact on who they are individually, and what the business is. There have been stories about people who founded and led the family, who are not with us anymore, but who still show up in our daily life.

Sometimes, those stories come as a surprise. Chris recently heard one such story from his father, which he had never heard before and neither had his sister. It shows the importance of being intentional about recognizing and sharing those little things.

So, sweat the small things. Pay attention to them. Not in a negative way. Take those small things and turn them a positive. Little things can have a big impact on so many aspects of your life.

TAKEAWAYS FROM THIS CHAPTER

Little things can be a big deal. The small details in any relationship can have a huge significance. Paying attention to those little things takes a lot of time and effort, but the payoff is big because it shows how much you care.

- How can you communicate "I see you, hear you, love you, and appreciate you" to your spouse and kids?
- Do you have recent wins that you celebrated? If you didn't celebrate them, why not?
- Do you speak "love language" to your spouse and kids? Is what you say to them and how you say it meaningful to them?

5

PARENTING WITH GOD IN MIND

It's funny how an unexpected complication can lead to something positive. We had some travel issues that resulted in us spending seven hours together in the car. We spent part of that time listening to an audio book, *You and Me Forever* by Francis Chan, and one specific chapter led to this chapter in our book. It's about parenting with God in mind.

Let's start with God's opinion of children. It comes from Psalm 127:3-5, and it says, "*Behold, children are a heritage from the Lord, the fruit of the womb, a reward. Like arrows in the hand of a warrior are the children of one's youth. Blessed is the man who fills his quiver with them. He shall not be put to shame when he speaks with the enemies in the gate."*

But have you noticed that over the last 30 years or so, there's been an attitude shift about large families? For the longest time, large families were looked upon as a blessing. Of course, there was a practical reason for that. With so many family farms, having a lot of kids meant you had a lot of help on the farm.

Now, having more children is often considered more of a burden. There's extra expense, added responsibility, loss of freedom. When people see a large family, they often wonder, "What were they thinking?"

Francis speculates that one reason we see children as a burden is because of how they show up, which makes a lot of sense. Using the reference of a quiver full of arrows, he says, "But a bunch of crooked arrows or unruly kids meant it would come back to haunt you." So, what's causing that shift in the way kids show up? What makes them disrespectful, pushing back on authority in a big way? It really boils down to parenting.

Which brings us to the question of what parenting with God in mind looks like. What does it look like if we say, "We're going to parent like God calls us to parent?"

What makes a great parent? Is it a parent that does everything for their children? Or is it a parent that actually trains the child to do for themselves? Training is part of raising a child. From the early years of toilet training and teaching them to tie their shoes to all the things they need to know to be ready for life. Can they do laundry? They're going to need to do that when they're out on their own. We've been very clear with our children that our goal is to make ourselves obsolete in the daily tasks, but always available when needed.

Sometimes you have to look back a generation. People who struggle with parenting are often replicating what they lived in many ways. You typically do what you know. Often, people just don't know anything different.

But you have to be very mindful, if what you're doing is what you know and it's not working, you're going to have to step outside of that and ask for help or seek other ways. Which is difficult. It's admitting weakness. But where do you want your heart to be?

There are parents that just want to make life as comfortable as possible for their kids. Sometimes their motivation is the desire to be liked or needed or thanked or praised, or to have the child think of them as a friend. But that's doing a big disservice to the child. They're not learning to be self-sustaining and self-sufficient.

Which leads to this question: Do we want to help create a blessing to the world or a burden to the world? Not helping your children become self-sustaining is creating a burden. One which will just go on and on. Kids learn early, if they cry somebody pays attention. Sometimes that crying goes on into adulthood, and sometimes parents still pay attention. But that's enabling your child. You're not teaching them how to be effective. They're a burden, not a blessing. Rather than carrying a quiver full of arrows, it's filled with unsharpened sticks. They'll never leave the quiver. They'll never find their mission and purpose in life. They won't even get challenged to find it. Why would they? You're doing everything for them.

Our youngest is 14, and she has a lot of life left to figure things out, which we're consistently encouraging her to do. Our older two, who are 23 and 19, have both used their life experiences and struggles as learning tools to try to be a blessing moving forward. Both have a big desire to show up as a picture of

Jesus. If you ask them about how they want to serve and how they want to show up, it's very specifically helping other people overcome the struggles that they've had, and showing how their faith has led them to overcome that struggle. Not taking credit for overcoming the struggle, but saying, "I was able to overcome that struggle because I learned to lean on the Lord." That's how they show up.

That's something you have to learn. As a parent, you want your child to have purpose in life. But if you force feed them a mission and responsibility, how do they figure out how to show up? However, if they become self-aware, they start doing the hard work of figuring out how to show up differently. They find a purpose in the mission and take on responsibility.

We always knew we were going to raise our children to be God-fearing. That's creation of disciples. An important thing that Francis touched on in the book is having kids that love Jesus more than they love us, which can be a hard thing to think about. But on the flip side of that, when you have a child, you're stewarding them. They don't belong to you.

Having children see that you love God more than them, gives them a picture of what their life should be, that they should love God more than their kids. They should love God more than their spouse. It's truly putting Him first. Francis uses himself as an example. He's a pastor and he serves all over the world. But when he's away from home, his children understand he's doing it because of the way he loves the Lord and the burden he has for people. There's no animosity, there's no hurt feelings. They just know, "It's okay because that's what we all should be doing. It's normal to do that."

Kids know when you're faking it. They know when you're lukewarm. There's actually a younger generation that's leaving the church because they're resentful of lukewarm parents. They realize, "Loving Jesus means something. It's not just being lukewarm in your home, not putting family before God." That's a problem. And in the homes where family is put before God, then the majority of the kids leave the church at 18. They see incongruities. "You're saying one thing, you're doing another, particularly when it comes to me."

They can see if you're just dialing it in. They can see when we're not living up to what we say. If we're telling them, "I love God more than I love you, and that's the way it should be. You should be loving the Lord more than me," then ask yourself, what would break your heart the most? If your children didn't love you, or if your children didn't love Jesus? That would be a difficult question for some people, but if you think it all the way through, if they love Jesus, they're going to love you. Francis says, "I've never met someone who loved Jesus, who did not love their parents."

We talked earlier about kids showing up as being disrespectful to their teachers or disrespectful to authority figures. All of that disrespect is something that they're catching. They're seeing a lack of respect, which would lead them to not respect God's authority, because He's just another authority. "What gives Him the right to give me a command? What gives Him the right to demand that I be obedient? It's not comfortable to me, so I don't want to participate in that. So, just like every other authority in my life, I'm going to disrespect it."

How do you show respect in the home? How does respect show up? These are important questions to ask yourself. How do you show up to your kids? Do they understand that in your home you love Jesus first? How do you demonstrate that? What does respect mean in your home? How are you showing up?

We've told all three of our children, our job is not to be their friend. Our purpose is to make sure they can be "grown and flown". They can go out and be productive, they can contribute, they can live out their purpose. This sometimes rubs our children very much the wrong way, especially when it's one of those "this is for your own good" conversations.

Suzanne lived through this. When she went off to college, one of the girls she lived with came from a family where everything had been done for her. She didn't know how to function. She literally had no idea. Suzanne decided back then that she would never have a child who can't function outside their house. She knew she would have failed as a parent if that was the case. We both believe that. We would fail as parents if they can't survive and function and think and solve problems, and do all those things without us having to do it for them, or tell them how. Which sometimes means letting them fail, even fail epically.

Our mission as parents is to create disciples. There's currently an absolute attack on the church, which means it's going to get harder and harder to show up as a Jesus follower. The last thing we need is for them to not have the strength to withstand. We'd rather them learn to gather that strength while they are in our care. It's our job now to be there when they struggle, and show them the guidance to help get them through.

Our older daughters learned that, and now they want to serve based on the struggles they went through. God showed up for them, and that's what they want to get through to others. We helped them be able to do that because we put them in the right circles, introduced them to the right people, and gave them a firm foundation in their faith. That's how we parented. Now, as it gets harder to show up as a Jesus follower, they're going to have to have some backbone. If they're going to show up in the workplace like we're asking them to, they'll have to not only contribute to society instead of being a burden, they'll have to shine a light. They'll have to do their part to help create disciples.

How in the world could kids do that if they were coddled, even if they were raised in a Christian home? When they face a trial, if they haven't learned to lean, they're going to collapse under the weight of what they're facing. For us as parents, that's a massive failure.

Courage is cultivated. You're not born with it. You don't show up one day and automatically have it. Courage comes from knowing that you've faced adversity and come out the other side. You may not have come out unscathed, but you came out. And you learned and you put more tools into your tool bag so when you experience that again, you have something to draw from. Which is not that different than any other kind of stress or adversity that you might come against. But if you haven't started to cultivate that and work that muscle and really figure out how to do it and how to be resilient, you are going to crumble.

It's got to start somewhere. Foundations are so important. We hope we've given our daughters that foundation so when the time comes, they'll either figure it out themselves, or maybe have some people like them in their generation to shine the light and say, "Why don't we parent with God in mind? Let's start there."

One of the things we have to keep in mind as parents and adults is you are going to be attractive to people who see something in you that they either need or want or just are subconsciously drawn to. Sometimes it's your sense of calm, your sense of peace. Sometimes it's your strength, your courage in the face of adversity. So we don't think our kids are going to have a problem finding a way to serve, and finding a way to be that, because we can already see that people are drawn to them because of their inner qualities, not anything that people can necessarily visually see and touch. It's not tactile, but they just know there's something there that's different.

So, going back to the question of whether you love God more than your spouse or your children, or whether your children love God more than they love you, let's hope so. Because if we can get that part right, everything else takes care of itself.

If they love Jesus, they're going to love you. If they're a Christ follower, then the way they show up in the world will be so drastically different that it will be a beacon of light and cause a difference.

TAKEAWAYS FROM THIS CHAPTER

We all want to be the best parents possible to our kids. We all have a Father who can help us do that. It can come down to the difference between teaching our kids versus doing everything for them. One creates a blessing, the other a burden. One of the most important lessons you can teach them is how God comes first for you, as He should for them.

- How do you show up to your kids? Have you asked them?
- Do they understand that in your home you love Jesus first? What does that love look like?
- Do your kids understand that Mom/Dad comes first to the other before them?

6

GROUNDED IN GRATITUDE

What are you grateful for today? What were you grateful for yesterday? Did you even think about that?

Gratitude has always been very important to us. But it became very clear to us thanks to an unusual habit Chris developed a few years ago. On March 15, 2020, the day everything pretty much shut down due to Covid, he began getting up at sunrise, walking outside our house, and just standing on the lawn reflecting on things. He's barefoot, and does that no matter the weather. In fact he's been out there in nine inches of snow.

He learned about this at an event Steve Weatherford hosted in Utah called Upgrade Your Human, which involved spending three days doing things as a tribe. That included Wim Hof breathing. If you're not familiar with that, you should learn about it. It can do so much for your body and your mind.

The Wim Hof instructor was named Dr. Trish and what she taught was life-altering. In addition to the breathing, there was a lot of exposure to the cold, including things like ice baths and hiking a mountain in the snow wearing just a pair of shorts. She showed how important this is in terms of gratitude and grounding. We'll explain both of those in a bit. But just putting your feet on the ground first thing in the morning, and getting into a circadian rhythm, can make a difference in your physical health as well as your mental well-being. This was important to Chris because of his family health history, including dementia, diabetes and heart disease.

Do you pay attention to your sleep patterns? Prior to that event, if you had asked Chris how much sleep he gets, the answer would have been four to five hours a night. His braggadocious response would be, "If you need more than that, you don't have enough to do." But when Dr. Trish talked with him about paying attention to his sleep, and she learned about his health history, she told him, "We're going to change your thought process." She asked him how much dream sleep he was getting, and he didn't know...maybe 30-45 minutes a night. She said, "Well, that's a problem."

You may monitor your deep sleep. But have you thought about your dream (REM) sleep? Chris now wears a WHOOP band, which gives him that answer. This is important because there have been several studies that say when you dream, your brain is getting a chemical flush that cleans the plaque and other issues that could potentially lead to brain malfunction later in life.

Dr. Trish had a long heart-to-heart talk with Chris about the importance of sleep and getting into a rhythm of the sunrise and sunset. You just have to spend two or three minutes, five minutes tops, watching the sunrise in the morning. And if the opportunity presents itself, watching it set at night. For Chris, these few moments every morning allow him to create a connection with God. He's putting his body, which was created by God, directly on the earth that God created. So it's also a spiritual experience.

Every day when he does this, he asks himself this question: "What's one thing today that I'm grateful for?" Which means he's figured out a lot of reasons to be grateful to be here. We all have those reasons; we just may not realize we do.

Sometimes the answer is the simplest thing. Sometimes it's complicated. Often, by doing this, it helps us later that day. If you're struggling with something, and your brain goes back to that thing you're grateful for, it shifts your mindset. We talk a lot about reaction versus response. This gives you a better ability to respond, and has changed the way Chris responds in many cases.

The other important thing he learned doing that is called "soft-focus hard-focus." You steady your breathing, pick something that's about 25 yards away, and intently focus on it. It needs to be something specific like a limb on a tree, or even a leaf. You do that and everything else should fade away. Then after about 30 seconds, you go into soft focus, which means you focus on nothing.

At first, he couldn't reach that point, but he learned that was because of his job running the car dealerships. She said, "All day, every day, you're looking for problems to solve or people are bringing you problems to solve. That means you're just doing hard focus all day long." So, she worked with him on it and he worked on it after the event, and then one day it clicked. Everything went fuzzy, then suddenly went clear again. This has also helped him tremendously in dealing with challenges, both at work and at home.

That early-morning routine…gratitude, focus, and connecting with God and the planet…has really been life-changing. When you can ground yourself, everyone around you will also reap the benefit.

Grounding, in its very basic form, is just allowing your body to have that moment of connection and release of negatives. That may sound odd, but here's a way to think about it. Picture yourself in the winter, when the air is really dry, and you're wearing a big fuzzy sweater and wool socks, and when you touch someone, you feel a spark. That is one of the two of you unloading that charge into the other person. The same thing happens when you put your feet in the dirt or in the grass or in nature in general. It just allows your body to release any energies that aren't going to serve you.

When you just walk outside with your feet in nature, regardless of the time of day, there's a sense of immediate calm that happens in your body. If you haven't tried that, you really need to because it's real. It's a very real thing.

It's very similar to when Suzanne does energy response testing or energy muscle testing with clients. Her body acts as a battery would to their body. If you put the positive ends together, they're going to push apart. If you put a positive and negative together, they're going to have a connection. It helps you to figure out what's going on physically. So, in very simple terms, just go get your feet dirty.

Gratitude and grounding both give your body a reset. This is one of the things Suzanne stresses a lot when working with people who are under a great amount of stress, whether it's self-imposed or things they can't control. Because when you practice gratitude, that is allowing for the good to creep in. it's very simple; when you start focusing on good, you start seeing more good.

When you put yourself into a situation where you are grounded or doing hard things, not that you necessarily have to do the hard things to get grounded, but if you can do those in conjunction, then your threshold for what is going to trigger you is going to be higher. Where you may have been at a 3, you might be at an 8 or 9 now. You're not going to spiral out. You're not going to end up quite as mentally negative as you would have before, because your threshold has been raised to a higher level. Then you get to reset because that's your new starting point. That's when you start looking for the good and understanding that anything you can do to raise that threshold is going to serve you very well in the long run. Just a few minutes will make a very big difference.

Many people have a hot tub at their house. We have an ice tub. It goes down to 37 degrees and stays there. At any given point, Chris can get in it. We know people who do this daily. We're thinking it could be a vital part of a weekly routine. No matter how often we use it, it's there for us when we need it.

This also stems from that event in Utah. One of the first things they did was go into an icy lake. The air temperature was 39 degrees and the water was about the same, and they all just walked into the water. Chris had been in an ice bath once before and it was a horrible experience, but this time he was shocked to find himself comfortable. How did his body adapt so quickly? It turns out that when you put your body in an intentional stressful situation like that, it adapts because it doesn't know the difference between the types of stresses, like work stress or things like that, and intentionally suffering in an ice bath. The physiological body response is identical. It allows you to handle those stressful situations that pop up.

Even one of our daughters has said she knows that an ice bath or a cold shower, something that puts her in a physically uncomfortable place, helps her deal with stress or anxiety.

You probably didn't expect a discussion about stress in a chapter about gratitude, but it's all connected. Our lives are stressful. Our jobs are stressful. That's going to lower your ability to soft-focus. But as you learn how to handle stress effectively, you're going to see that soft-focus becomes something you can routinely come in and out of.

Stress management is also a big part of Suzanne's work with her clients in the naturopath space. Our bodies react physically to stress. But when we can manage that response, we are helping ourselves physically, mentally, and emotionally.

So, are you actively practicing gratitude? It's one thing to just say, "I'm grateful," but it's something else entirely to actually do that deep dive every day, identify what you're grateful for, and express your gratitude for them. Now it's intentional.

The studies on this are fascinating. They looked at people who intentionally worked on gratitude versus those who didn't. They studied the elasticity of their brains. In other words, how their brain functioned. Their ability to learn new things, to handle change, to handle stress, along with the incidence of Alzheimer's and dementia, and all other brain cognitive functioning issues. In every one of those areas, there is a drastic difference in those who actively practice gratitude daily versus those that don't.

Longevity is a significant one. There's a drastic difference in how long they're able to function with full capacity. So there's a huge physiological reason to do this.

Think of this in terms of prayer. When you pray, you pray with adoration and confession and giving thanks, which is gratitude and supplication. So when you say "I am grateful for this," you're recognizing the source of those gifts. It can be a very deeply spiritual practice. For Chris, that moment of gratitude sets the tone for the whole day. It impacts him, and everyone around him.

TAKEAWAYS FROM THIS CHAPTER

We all have something to be grateful for, but we don't always think about it. Few people practice gratitude daily. If you do ask yourself what you're grateful for, sometimes the answer is simple and sometimes it's complicated, but it's always beneficial. Intentionally practicing gratitude can actually help you live longer and be healthier. When you ground yourself, you're able to release the negatives. You're able to give your body a reset.

- What stressors are you currently dealing with?
- Do you normally respond or react?
- Do you currently have a gratitude practice? If no, why not? If yes, how can you improve it?
- How do you reset when things aren't going well?

7

PURPOSE IN THE PAIN

This topic is the result of a couple conversations we've had with people we know who are dealing with pain. It can be tough to accept, or understand, but there is a purpose in pain. It can be very difficult to see that in the moment, but when we look back and see the trials and tribulations we've gone through, and the pain we've endured, and really take a closer look, hopefully we can see the purpose.

The first example is a friend who lost his wife about 10 years ago. The next-door neighbor of the woman he's dating was recently killed in a car crash. That woman's husband is obviously devastated. Chris shared with our friend that he'd be able to relate to that man in a way nobody else could, and maybe that could help him find purpose in his pain.

The widower is a reclaiming atheist. He has no belief in God. His wife was a believer. Before she died, their family had expressed concern that if something were to happen to her, he would never come to know Christ. As it turns out, through lots of conversations, he actually has started to attend the grief share group at our church, which is the perfect place for him. Without a group like this, how would he have dealt with the pain of his wife passing in this sudden, tragic way?

Without a test, there's no testimony. How often do we examine our lives and think about the pain we experienced and ask ourselves, "How can I use my pain point and the way God brought me through it to help someone else through a similar type of pain?"

We discussed this on a few of our podcast episodes, when we talked with couples who dealt with pain. For example, Jeff and Ali Wendt were both widowed when they met. Now they're married. It's part of their mission to really pour into other couples, to help them get through whatever they're dealing with. They made a very insightful statement during our conversation. "Grief is a season, it's not an identity." You could apply that to anything you're going through. It's temporary. It doesn't need to become who you are.

Brooke and Chadd Wright found purpose in a different type of pain. Brooke went through very severe drug addiction and recovery. As a result, there are people only she can reach, because she's lived it. She knows what it feels like. The same for Chadd. He knows what it's like to walk a spouse through that process, so only he would be able to reach a certain group of people. A lot of times there's community in problems, and we can use it for good or bad.

Many people have found purpose in the pain of addiction. One of Chris' best friends recently celebrated eight years sober. A while back, he was asked to be part of the leadership of his church's addiction program. He had some reservations about that, which he discussed with Chris.

He said, "When you're out there sharing, it's like standing up there naked because everybody gets to see all the struggle." Chris told him, "Yes, but you're going to be able to have that conversation with people in a way nobody else can, because you know you couldn't do it on your own. You needed to put the strength in God to get you through that. Once you did, and surrendered it to Him, you were able to overcome it."

He's talked very openly with Chris about his struggles, like he would with a sponsor. Chris has often told him, "I don't have this struggle and I don't know what it's like to walk in your shoes, but I'm always here if you want to talk about this."

If you look back at your individual struggles, ask yourself, "How did God bring me through that in that season? And how am I supposed to be using that to help other people who are struggling with that same thing?" One of the reasons we chose to do our podcast is to reach out to people that have come through things and put them on full display. By letting them share their story about coming through struggles and leaning on God to get them through it, people can hear it and say, "I'm not alone in that. Maybe that's my answer."

What helps with that on the individual side is listening to those moments where the Holy Spirit says to you, "Hey, that's somebody you need to touch." We don't mean physically. It's a feeling that you should just open your mouth and move forward in having a conversation. Are you listening when that happens?

Our pastor touched on this in one of his sermons. He said, "I know you heard what the pastor had to say, but did you hear what God had to say?" There are multiple ways to take that. Are you spending time alone with God listening to what He has to say? Are you spending time alone in His word? Are you doing more than listening to your pastor on Sunday morning? And even then, are you listening to what God's saying to you and not what the pastor's saying to you? Are you listening for the moments of, "Share this, speak to this person, evangelize." Are you listening to what God's saying when you're trying to help someone deal with pain? A nudge can be a very powerful thing.

One of the things they work on in the leadership development group at Chris' business is relationships. Every quarter, each person gets to pick one relationship they want to pour into. So, at the end of the year, there are four deeper relationships in their life. Often, they choose their spouse or a child. As a father of three, and having been married for 25-plus years, that's something Chris can speak to. How do you develop a deeper relationship with your spouse or child? How can be intentional with your relationship with them?

Often, the reason they want to work on that relationship is because it might be waning, or they feel like they're losing control. When Chris or someone else in the group tries to walk them through this, sometimes it involves using their own pain. In that moment, there's purpose in their pain, as they share with someone who's asking "How do I make it through this?"

Chris and his sister were talking about the leadership development group after one quarterly meeting, and Chris made this observation: a lot of people go in thinking it's some type of group therapy. But there's a drastic difference between therapy and coaching. With therapy, you're talking with somebody to help you walk yourself through a problem, whereas with this coaching, you're dealing with someone who has walked themselves through it. A therapist is trained to help you walk through your own problem, but a great coach has been in the situation and can let you learn from their own personal mistakes. It's a much more personal walk through it, because they are discussing the purpose in their pain. They're giving examples of the hard points, or sticking points of what you're developing.

There are times you want to tell people, "Just listen, so you don't have to do it the hard way." It's like when your parents tell you, "I've been there, I've done that. You're not going to have a good outcome if you do it that way." Unfortunately, most of the time you still do it that way, and it turns out your parents were right about the outcome. But sometimes people do come to a point of frustration, or the end of the rope, or they feel like it's going down into what we call circling the drain, because it's just not going anywhere positive.

Sometimes you can help those people without having to share with them, just by being present and letting them unload on you. Because you've been through hard things, you're able to be that strong presence. If they're falling apart, you can speak life back into them. Another couple on our podcast, Derrick & Ilya Golden, said they wanted to love people back into their life, and they're helping them learn to live again. Discipleship isn't always clean. Sometimes what you've learned through your life lessons is very dirty, but you might need to get in the ditch and be dirty with somebody else so you can help walk them back through the process. Because when people get to that point, a lot of times what they don't have is hope.

So, knowing the struggles we've been through, are we looking for the opportunity to use those struggles to bring others to Christ? Are we using this as a discipleship tool? People often see their testimony as how they came to know Christ or came to their faith. But if that's where the story ends, then people get the misconception that when that happens, everything gets easy. But for the vast majority, it gets harder.

The desire to live differently is there. It requires a different vantage point, a different lens on life. We need to be open to that and saying, "This is my moment of recognizing I need a savior in my life. Because of that recognition, I had something that brought me through my challenges other than just my own sheer strength and will. That's why I needed Jesus."

It is all the purpose and the pain and all the struggles that we go through. And it creates community. Both a sense of community and a true community, because you're not meant to do it by yourself. You're not meant to go it alone. If we were more mindful of being in that community, and engaging with that community frequently and consistently, the problems we tend to find would probably be caught and quit far faster.

You get some perspective. It gives perspective to what you're going through if you're hearing somebody else that's walked it. It gives you hope to see someone who's made it through it and is now thriving. Everyone loves an underdog story, but when you think about it, the underdog story is almost always how someone has a moment of pain and rises above it. The difference in our underdog story is we don't rely just on our own ability to pull ourselves up. It's about recognizing the fact that we couldn't do it by our own strength. And the minute we stopped trying to do it by our own strength, that's when we were pulled through.

We've talked about our own personal struggles a few times in this book. The first time we went to Christian-based couples therapy, it gave us such a different perspective on many things, including what love is. Going through that, and then talking to others about where we were individually and as a couple, the struggles we went through, and how we got through them and emerged stronger, gives purpose to our pain.

It's certainly not fun to look back at that struggle, but if we had not gone through that, we wouldn't have experienced faith-based counseling, and been able to share that with others who have also come out stronger. We would have preferred not to go through the pain. Given a choice, who wouldn't? But there are many positives that came out of it. There was a purpose to it.

It helped us, and in turn, we've been able to help others. As an extension of us walking through it, we've been able to point others in a direction and then they were able to move in a very positive way. Like the man we mentioned at the beginning of this chapter whose wife was killed. Because of our friend, he's giving an example of how God showed up for him. As we said, this is a man who says "I don't even believe there is a God". But he's willing to step foot in a church and have conversations with people who have experienced the same type of grief he's experienced, which will give purpose to their pain. By extension, that is how you meet people where they are, with no agenda, no judgment. They just love you and you love them.

This chapter may lead you to do some self-reflection. If you're a couple and have experienced some struggles, do some self-reflection about those struggles and how you came through them, and ask yourself, "How can we, as a couple, help others with our pain?" The same holds true if you're single. If you're struggling or have struggled, and you came through it, what was the source of your strength? If you know that it was something much bigger than you, you're able to share that with someone as part of a testimony. Not just how you came to Christ, but how He showed up for you. How God showed up for you. How the Holy Spirit speaks to you.

It's all those things, and it gives purpose to your pain.

We mentioned our podcast several times in this chapter. If you'd like to subscribe to the show, or just listen to an episode, scan the QR code:

TAKEAWAYS FROM THIS CHAPTER

When you're dealing with pain, whether that's physical or emotional, it can be difficult to see past that moment and even more difficult to accept that there is a purpose in that pain. But without a test, there's no testimony. You can use your pain point and the way God got you through it to help others dealing with something similar. Even if you can't relate to someone else's struggle, sharing what God has done for you can be helpful. There's community in problems, which we can use for good or bad.

- How can you meet people where they are and love them well?
- How have you come through a hard season? What was your "saving grace"?
- What did you learn? What can you share now?
- How can you better respond to nudges from God to take action?

8

DEFINING SUCCESS

Success is very subjective. Everyone's vision is different. The two of us have different views of what success is in different areas, whether that's our marriage or our family or Chris' business. So it's important that when you're leading in a conversation, it's always a good idea to ask the other person what their vision, their definition, their version of success looks like. And get detailed. What does it look like? What does it feel like? What are you wearing? Where are you standing? Get really clear on their version of success.

Suzanne does this a lot in her coaching, and she's found that most people have never even thought about their definition of success. When she's in her first session with new clients, this is the first thing they talk about. And most of the time, they don't know what success looks like. They don't know where they want to go, because they've never thought about what the end looks like.

Let's put this in the context of something many people can relate to: weight loss. People may know they want to lose 20 pounds, but they don't think about what that looks like for them. Will they feel successful beyond achieving a goal? What will they be able to do? What aspects of their life are different and better? Will their relationships be different and better? We try to look at it from all angles.

People often use their weight as a crutch. "I can't do that because I need to lose 20 pounds." But then, when the crutch has been removed, they may still not want to do that. So it's never about one thing. But when you can help someone get really excited about the end results and what that success looks like, you're far more able to get them to set goals and have conversations around things that are much more meaningful to them.

Suzanne may see tremendous potential in people in certain areas, so she wants to push that agenda because she sees them as having the ability, but they have no interest in that. They won't see that as success, so it's not going to be meaningful to them. It's not going to matter. That's why they always have to define it. Then, as their provider, she has to honor that even if she doesn't agree with it.

This has played a role in the leadership development work Chris has been doing at his business. They talk a lot about vision, because many people believe they're good at defining objectives and tactics, but they can't envision what the end result looks like. What's the vision of success? Can they write that down? Part of this process involves having people write down a statement. "I will become this. I will have this." They work on their relationship space, their contribution space, and their mind and spirit space. How would they vision out the success of their relationships? For many people, this is the first time they've been presented with questions about how all this would look to them.

But if they can write it down and make it a clear statement, every day the tactic gets a little easier, because the tactic is not about the objective anymore, it's about who they're becoming through the tactic. Many times, when they see the objective, they not only achieve it faster than they imagined, they actually overachieve what they thought they would be able to do.

Let's talk about this in the context of marriage. Have you asked your spouse, "What does success in marriage look like to you?" Ideally that's a question you should ask before you get married, and certainly make it an ongoing conversation during marriage. It should be revisited pretty often, because what you envisioned as success at a certain point in your marriage likely looks very different than what actually came to fruition.

There are two ways you can fail in this. Maybe you have a clear idea of what you perceive as success and what success looks like to you. You can be dead set on it, and never veer from it, in which case you don't have a life. On the flip side, as soon as you hit something that's difficult, that gets you off track or off course or just disillusioned, you kind of throw it away and at that point your vision is lost. You don't have one anymore. It's very important to have that conversation frequently.

In our case, what we will see as success for our second child in college, is going to be very different than what we saw for our eldest. How we manage the success of the next few years is going to have to be an ongoing conversation. What each of us sees as success not only may be different than the other's vision, it may be out of our realm of understanding. So we have to be careful to understand each other's idea of success and pour into that while not pushing what we may see.

When Suzanne talks about this with her clients, and gets them started on this path, she encourages them to write everything down. She calls it a brain dump. Whatever pops into your head, write it down. It doesn't have to have rhyme or reason, order, columns, categories. If you're super organized, you're going to have to get outside your box for a minute, but just write down every single word that comes to mind. Give yourself a time limit, maybe two minutes, and then go back and group things together. You'll find that there are patterns once you start looking at those words. Do that individually and then do it together. Share with your spouse and see what's in common. Start there. If you start with what's in common, it's going to be far easier than trying to chase two separate dreams, because that kind of defeats the purpose. Yes, you want to have your own, but if you're doing it with a spouse, with no kids, with no other obligations at the moment, find those commonalities and grow those. Be flexible because things are not going to be simple, or easy, or go in a straight line.

As we mentioned earlier, when Suzanne has her first session with a new client, the first thing she asks them is what success looks like for them. She can get them there quicker if she knows where they're going. Then she can help them figure out the three or four things that need to happen in order for them to get there. But of course, not everything is going to go perfectly, so the next question is, "What are three things that could get in your way? What are three things you could do to overcome each of those things?"

Then the last question is what are their non-negotiables? What are they not willing to try, or change? What won't they give up? A lot of times their non-negotiables are 100% what keeps them from reaching that success vision. They're getting in their own way. But when she works with them on shifting one of those non-negotiables, even just a little bit, it starts them down that road towards success. Maybe they make another shift the next week. It's a matter of degrees. Make one small change, master it, make another small change, master it. If you do that once a week, every week for an entire year, you've changed 52 things. That would be substantial.

Bear in mind, people typically don't like change. They don't like to have to critically evaluate what they're currently doing because most of the time it's comfortable for them. And even if someone does get on a good path, if they run into adversity, it's very likely they're going to go back to something that is comfortable. We're just creatures of habit in that way.

You have to allow people coming along with you to do that at their own pace. They'll get on this path when they're ready. But some people will never be ready. They'll fight you the whole way and never be a convert. On the other hand, if you give them a couple weeks, some people will see that you're being steadfast in it, and the curiosity will get the better of them. They'll jump on board because they want to see what it's about, but also because they're seeing things which they might not have seen you as being capable of. Now you're being capable. You're going to force them to reevaluate, and possibly dream on their own. It builds their trust. If they see you having success, they begin to trust the process.

This brings us back to the leadership work Chris is doing. When they work on relationships, they break them down into 12-week cycles, and they encourage people to be really intentional about what that relationship will look like in 12 weeks. What steps are they going to take every week during that time? What tactics will they use? Where do they want that relationship to be? How will their partner hold them accountable?

Then, as the 12 weeks unfold, what wins have they achieved? There's almost always something that never would have happened prior to the conversation about what they want to grow into. It's so important for them to recognize and celebrate those wins, even the littlest ones. That recognition builds the trust of the process.

Recognizing the non-negotiables is a key part of this. They may not have a good reason for holding onto them, but when they write them down, they're taking ownership of them. It's an emotional attachment. They don't want to let them go. But as their mindset shifts over time, these non-negotiables become negotiable. Instead of being unwilling to give up negatives, now they're willing to try new things. They shift from holding on to trying something new and eventually letting go.

This also plays a role in your faith. How do we figure out what God says is success for us? You have to be willing to put aside what you think 10 years or 20 years down the road is going to look like, and appreciate your gifting, your calling, what you're able to contribute, where you can pour in and invest.

If you can turn over the need to be in the driver's seat, success is inevitable. You are going to be successful because you're taking the ownership and giving it to somebody else. "I'm just going to walk in this path. I'm going to walk in my gifting, I'm going to walk in my calling, I'm going to walk where I can invest. I'm going to serve; I'm going to pour in." You're going to be successful because it's a shift in who's driving and what the reward is.

Bruce Wilkinson wrote a book called *The Dream Giver*. It starts out as a parable about Nobody. An ordinary person from Nowhere. Towards the end of the parable, the dream giver says, "Now give me your dream. I've placed it in you. Now you have to give it to me." Which is one of the stumbling blocks most of the time, because we want to be in control of that more often than not. If we look at true success, massive success is always unexplainable other than God has his hand in it. You have to do the work, but God's going to meet you where you give out. It pays huge dividends when people can understand this in a relationship in their own personal life, and are able to impart this to their children. When you realize that you have to do all you can, but the real success is going to shine through where God steps in.

So, going back to where we started and wrapping this up, let's define what success looks like with vision. It means painting a picture as vividly as possible. Get specific. Know the details, down to what color is your underwear? Then write it down, and share it. Because it's not a vision if you don't share it with others.

Share it so other people can hold you accountable to it. Especially those that are in your immediate circle, like your spouse and your children. Bear in mind, when you do share it, because it's going to be something they've never done before, they're going to have a tendency to want to slow you down because they don't want you to be disappointed. They're going to limit how big you can dream.

But write it down, share it with someone to help hold you accountable, and revisit it often.

TAKEAWAYS FROM THIS CHAPTER

Success means different things to different people. For many, it's materialistic. But often, little victories mean more than big bucks. Sometimes, you have to sacrifice something to get where you want to be, but always be aware of the things that are just too important to give up.

- What does success look like for you?
- What do you need to do?
- What is going to get in your way?
- What are your non-negotiables?

9

CONFLICTS ARE ESSENTIAL

To have a successful marriage, you and your spouse can't have any conflicts, right? Wrong! Conflicts are actually essential.

We can't take credit for this concept. It comes from Ray Dalio. You may know him as the founder of Bridgewater, but many people know him from his book, *Principles of Life and Work*, which really dives deep into culture principles. This quote was one of his principles of the day.

There are actually two factors to this. Conflicts are essential for great relationships because first, they're how people determine whether their principles are aligned, and second, it's how they resolve their differences.

Often, when people hear the word conflict, it brings about negative imagery. Their first thought is usually this means an argument. But it's really the best, or even the only way, to see whether you and the people that are in your circle have alignment in your principles. If you do, are there still differences? Where do they come from? The only way to resolve those is by getting them out in the open and on the table.

In American culture today, there's often a hesitancy to speak out because you're either going to hurt somebody's feelings, or you're going to be ostracized and kicked out of society as a whole because culture as a whole doesn't want their feelings hurt. There's an unwillingness to have conflict. "It's too uncomfortable. I don't want to be a part of that." But this is like friction. There has to be a little bit of a rub in order for anything to get polished. If you want to get better or you want to have something that is greater than what you're currently doing or sitting in, you're going to have to get uncomfortable. Friction creates discomfort, but you have to be okay doing that. If more people were willing to put aside preconceived notions, put aside what they think they know and talk about things in an open arena, they just might find they're far more alike than they are different.

Which brings us back to conflict in marriage. Some believe that divorce can come from conflict that's unresolved or unapproached or untapped. When they say there are irreconcilable differences, how many of those differences started out early in the marriage or even prior to the marriage? How many couples have deep dive conversations to recognize where there's alignment of principles? One benefit of premarital counseling is the idea of, "Let's come together with a third party and figure out how we align, or whether we align with where we're trying to go." If that practice takes place, that could be the baseline to come back to if there are issues, and say, "We said we aligned with this. Where did it go sideways?"

We have to admit, we haven't always been great at resolving conflict. But we have less of it at this point in our marriage. Is that because we're more aligned in our principles? Have we resolved our differences? We're certainly not afraid to hurt each other's feelings. We're very open with each other. That's because we both know that the other person is coming at us with raw feelings that are legitimate and/or from a place of love.

Remember, conflict isn't fighting. You can disagree. You can have different viewpoints and perspectives. The perfect example of that is that Suzanne is very risk averse. Chris is a risk taker. We're never going to align in that area. But if Chris' risk tolerance doesn't put anyone in our family in harm's way, or in danger of not having a roof over our heads, even though Suzanne isn't always comfortable with it, she's accepting of it. If you and your spouse don't agree on something like this, it doesn't mean it has to divide you or drive a wedge between you.

We've been married more than 27 years and together 30 years. That's a lot of years of stepping in the ditch, but then being able to get out of that ditch through open communication and continual conversation.

That also means consulting with each other instead of just moving forward with your own agenda. Here's a story we look back on now and laugh about, but it wasn't funny when it happened. We had been married just a few months when Chris left the house on Sunday afternoon and came home with a motorcycle. He pulled into the driveway and boom, instant conflict.

Let's give you some context on that. We had lived with Chris's parents for a bit while our house was being finished. And Suzanne was not working at the time. She was back in graduate school. So in short order we experienced marriage, living with parents, moving into our house, and life/career change. That's a lot. It was a huge transitional season of our life. Everything was up in the air, and we were just waiting for things to fall down on us.

Buying a motorcycle was a big financial decision with no discussion. Just, "Hey honey, I'm home. Check this out." That wasn't fair to Suzanne. Now, she'll be the first to say she wouldn't have said no to the decision. But she needed to be part of it. That was a major conflict. But something like that hasn't happened since then.

How do you make conflict work properly in your marriage? It starts with having the conversation. You need to be willing to hear the conflict, and participate in it. If you're the one that's been wronged, that means having the ability to handle the conversation and not be offended. Right now the world is, "Hey, I can't offend anybody." Yes, everybody has an equal voice. But the idea of everybody having their own truth is ridiculous. There is only one truth.

Bear in mind, being offended is a choice. You can very clearly choose whether you allow someone's words to affect you and how much power you're going to allow those words to have over you and in your life.

But how do you get to the point of being able to have those conversations and the conflicts without the fear of offending? You have to have some ground rules of how you're going to handle conflict. Weaponizing actions, weaponizing words, making someone feel shame over something is never okay. Because at that point, you're attacking the person in their personhood versus what you are taking offense from. If there is an action that needs to be addressed, then address that action. But don't make it personal so you're conveying your opinion and your thoughts of that action onto the person. Don't make that person feel that's who they are, and that's how you see them.

People do things they would really like to take back all the time. Once it's done, you can't. But that doesn't mean taking what happened or was said and becoming that person. If that's how you see that person, you're not fighting fairly. That's not having conflict that's going to make you better and resolve the difference. You're just going to end up continuing to make it more and more venomous. You're going to end up hurling things at each other that are going to be very harmful and hurtful and cut deep and probably won't be forgotten. Maybe even to the point where because it is so personal and so deep, there's no resolution there.

Often, when we discuss things like this, we're reminded of things we heard from the couples we interviewed on our podcast. For example, Steve Weatherford told us that one of the best things he got from some coaching was, "You have to give up the right to be right." And when Chadd and Brooke Wright spoke so openly about Brooke's drug addiction and the grace with which Chadd dealt with it, he said this: "I didn't put the addiction on her. I didn't see her as the addiction. I saw the addiction for what it was. So it was easier to handle that situation with grace."

Giving up the right to be right is a real challenge sometimes in conflict resolution. And it can be so important to display enough grace that you're not taking the situation and identifying the other person as who they are because of a dumb action they took. "That's not who you are. You're better than that."

One of the things that served us well in handling conflict, or even bringing conflicts to the surface so we could talk about them, is doing therapy. Earlier we mentioned premarital counseling, and the idea of having that third person in the room. Whether they're mediating or facilitating or even serving as the referee, that helps you work through the conflict.

It's fair to say that when there's conflict, in most cases, both people go into it thinking they're 100% right. Or they're trying to seek validation, or justification. Sometimes that starts with just a simple misunderstanding.

Recently we were in the kitchen with Avery, our oldest daughter. We were not communicating well. We would each say something to the other, and we would both say, "You're not understanding me." Then Avery said to us, "You're saying the same thing. You both are literally saying the same thing, but you're using different words." (Remember we did say counseling was a thing and this is one way we used it - to get on the same page with our words.)

A lot of times, that's where conflict starts. It's just not having the ability to hear what is being said, in a way that is conveying what's being said. That may be a circular way of describing it. But think of it this way. You can say something to your spouse. They hear you, but when they repeat it back to you, they're doing that with their voice, and how their brain is processing it. Your brain isn't hearing it the same way. So one or both of you could assume the other isn't hearing you. But they are. Loud and clear. They're just processing it differently.

It's important to understand that it doesn't have to be vocalized in the exact same speech in order for you to be on the same page. You're on the same level. You're in the same field. You're reading from the same book. Sometimes you just need that third person, whomever that might be, to step in and say, "Okay, time out. You're both saying the same thing. Now use language that you both understand."

We should point out, we had a conflict in front of our daughter, and that was okay. What you don't want to do is fight in front of your children. But if they're able to see you display grace, and giving up the right to be right, if they can see you resolve conflict, the picture it paints for them is that even when there's a disagreement, that doesn't mean it's the end all. That helps them as your children, and it will help them in their own marriage down the road.

We're often in a disposable society. Too many times, someone says, "Okay, if the marriage doesn't work, we can dispose of it and I can go on to the next one." Think how beneficial it can be if your kids see you resolve conflict in a healthy way, to work through emotions and disagreements, to have discussions and come to a resolution of differences. The funny thing is neither of us can even remember what we were discussing, we just remember the resolution.

Craig Groeschel, the senior pastor of Life Church, made a good point about this on his podcast. He said, "I think the problem with why we're so comfortable in not trying to work through things is because we've gotten to the habit of, 'Well, we're not going to do it God's way. We're not going to go into it as the covenant that it is. It's just a contract.'" And contractual things are typically pieces of paper, and they come out of distrust.

He used the example of drawing up a contract with someone who's going to do repairs at your house. You're trying to limit your liability and responsibility while making sure the work gets done, and they're just trying to make sure that once the work is done, they get paid. All of that doesn't really communicate that you believe the other one isn't actually going to go through with it unless you put it on paper. He said, "Unfortunately, if you're looking at your marriage in that same way, then it's just a piece of paper. So why get married?"

Which leads to people living together prior to marriage. Then they end up not just sharing space and sharing bills, but maybe sharing pets and then sharing kids, and then sharing all these other things. And then something happens and they're no longer satisfied. So they break up and move on. That's also their default if they do get into a marriage and conflict arises.

"I'm just going to break up and move on." Breaking up and moving on creates a perpetual cycle of people bringing more and more baggage into the next marriage or relationship, and the next one after that.

It would be so much better if instead of giving up and moving on, they would say, "I'm going to actually sit in it for a minute and figure out where this came from." Because we all bring baggage. We all bring things that are unresolved. And they need to be resolved if you're going to have a successful marriage.

Marriage isn't a piece of paper. It's a covenant. And it doesn't have to be conflict free. You can have many conflicts. You just need to be able to resolve them.

TAKEAWAYS FROM THIS CHAPTER

For many couples, conflict has a very bad connotation. But conflict doesn't mean fighting. It can actually help to determine alignment, and how to resolve differences. But be aware how much words matter, and be sure to use a language you both understand.

- Do you know how to fight fair?
- How can you approach your spouse when something hard needs to be discussed? Have you asked them for help with this?
- Are you able to give up the right to be right?
- Remember, marriage is a covenant, not a contract.

10

PROCESSES & RESPOND VERSUS REACT

It's no secret that successful businesses have good processes in place. That way, everyone knows what comes after what, and respond accordingly. That's especially valuable when something pops up that's not inside that process. Because when you don't have a process in place, when those crazy things do come up, you tend to react instead of respond, and you usually do that out of emotion, not practicality.

So, shouldn't it be the same for a family? Shouldn't you have processes in place so you can respond instead of react?

Let's use Chris' business as an example. Automobile dealers are very customer-centric. The customer's experience is critical. If there's no process in place, a customer's experience can depend on who they interact with, and how that person's day is going.

All of Chris' dealerships have a process which starts the moment a customer walks in the door. Whoever faces that customer knows just how to meet and greet them. They assess the customer's needs so those needs can be met promptly and properly. If someone's looking for a car, they need transportation. If they come in for service, they need a repair or maintenance. Assess the need, identify the issue, offer solutions, solve the problem, and then follow up. Most dealers do that, but we're aware that there are many pieces to the process, and we keep them very simple to take out as many variables as possible.

If the process is not followed appropriately, whether that's because it wasn't communicated well or understood, it violates our purpose statement, which is to enrich every life we touch by providing an incredible dealership experience. But if it does go south, we can identify where and how that happened. Sometimes company processes evolve as a result. On occasion we've learned that the process wasn't as simple as we thought.

If you get over processed, that can wreak as much havoc as not having a process.

That's the business aspect. How can you make that work in your family life?

Let's start with your faith. It means having a set routine of how you structure what you're going to do for your alone time, your quiet time, your devotion time, whatever you call it. It's how you process things during that time, and the fact that you're accountable to yourself for doing that on a daily basis. The problem comes when you miss a day, and it turns into a couple days, or a week, and next thing you know everything else starts falling apart because when you don't follow the process, you're violating your purpose. That being said, grace is important. Things come up in our lives. If you miss a day, forgive yourself for doing that, but make sure you're back on track the next day. Or even try to make it up later that day.

But try to have it scheduled every day. That structure really helps the process to work. Chris walks our dog every morning, and he uses that as a big part of his quiet time. That's when he listens to a devotional, and takes it in. It's a time to worship. It helps him start his day the best way possible.

The faith aspect of this is very personal. It can be very peaceful. On the other hand, the family aspect involves other people. It can be loud and it can be complicated. Just like in a business, you're factoring in different people with different personalities and different priorities and different opinions, all under one roof.

In our family, we have processes for how things are going to get handled, and what our response will be. For example, discipline. How do you discipline your children? What does that look like? Are you and your spouse in agreement on how you're going to do that?

We make sure we always present a unified front. We're always talking about discipline. Those conversations started before we had kids. We talked about how we grew up and how we were disciplined. We learned we came from very similar value systems, and we were disciplined pretty much the same way as children. As parents, we both have the same mindset in this area. We constantly tell our kids, we're not here to be their best friend. We're here to prepare them to be productive in life.

That doesn't mean we're satisfied with where we're at. We can still grow in this area. We're still evolving, and still asking questions like, "What are the roles and responsibilities of everybody in the household that have to be done on a daily basis? If something gets ignored, what does that look like? What are the consequences? What are the lasting results that will shift so they understand that there are responsibilities that are due?" Like many parents, we teach our kids that the chores they do every day make up the rent that's due to live under this roof. It's their part of lifting the load.

Our family dynamic is complicated. Our middle daughter went off to college, but our oldest moved back home after graduating college. She's now in seminary getting her Master of Divinity and working full-time. Our youngest is 14, and like many kids her age she's busy with school and sports. In fact, she probably spends less time home than any of us.

But despite everyone's schedules, or perhaps because of it, there's a lot that needs to get done in our house every day. For example, we don't eat out much. We cook a lot. On any given day, four different people are preparing three meals. That's 12 meals a day going through our kitchen. Which means a lot of dishes need washing every day. Who does them, and what happens if they don't get done? That's constantly evolving.

It's important to understand that whatever you decide to do in your home, in your family, it has to be dynamic. It's constantly going to shift and change based on what's going on with all the members of your household. You need to have the ability to know when a response is required, and what that response needs to be.

Another significant area where a process is important is the household budget. Nearly two thirds of American households live paycheck to paycheck, and it's not just lower-income households. There are plenty of families you would consider wealthy who would be in serious trouble if a paycheck went away. They don't have the ability to manage what's coming into the household. That's because they don't sit down and have a conversation about processing the income.

This is one of the reasons people don't tithe, or give to worthwhile organizations, or don't invest. They never sat down and said, "How can we make this work?" If you can find a good tool to use for that, it would pay huge dividends for you.

Going back to Chris' business for a moment, they evaluate their key performance indicators (KPI's) every week. Those numbers provide quantified results of how the business is doing. Then once a quarter, they look back at what they achieved and what they missed, and why those happened. That allows them to re-examine their processes. That's the point. You try, and if you fail, you learn and then you try again. If you succeed, you replicate it and share it, and test it and then try again.

How often do you reevaluate your household budget? For that matter, do you do it at all? That should be done at least every six months. With household chores, you may want to make an adjustment every 90 days, or even once a month. There should be a pulse to looking at the processes to make sure that everybody understands what's going on and what's trying to be achieved. It's a communication of vision.

We even have a process for our date nights. It's a great time for us to check in on a bunch of things. How are the kids doing? Is there something they're struggling with, whether that's grades or sports or something else? Is there a subject or a need or something that needs to be assessed?

And of course, checking in with each other and asking things like, "What's going on with you? How can I support you? Is there an area where you feel you need to reach out beyond our relationship to get enriched? Is there something going on spiritually that you need intercession for?"

One of the most important questions we ask each other is, "Is there a way you can find that I could serve you better?" Or, looking back, "Is there something that's already been going on that I could have served you better in?" Because again, it's that learn and fail process. If you're failing in it, how do you learn to do it better?

We still have plenty of date nights that are just fun, but some of them are very productive. Those are the ones where we go in with the attitude, this is how we're going to examine the areas. Does one of our daughters need special attention this week? What's on everyone's calendar? Is there a challenge where we need to make an adjustment so everyone's needs will be met?

It means going to date night with intention. Date night is not just going out for a steak dinner or a movie. It's about examining one another and asking how we pour into one another. Yes, it's important for us to have that nice dinner, and have this time by ourselves, but it serves a larger purpose in our relationship because it is about measuring the pulse of our family and measuring the processes of our family and seeing how we can serve one another better.

We talked about failing forward. Learning from your failures. It also helps to be able to look at a failure as a win. Let's explain that. If you find your process and never do a reevaluation, you're just saying, "This is the way it's going to be," which is really ineffective. But if you keep your eyes open to the fact that processes may change, and somewhere along the way your process breaks and fails, do you have ability to look at that as a win? No, it didn't work, but it's still a win because now you know that's not the way you need to continue. Knowing what not to do is as important as knowing what to try next. You have to fail and then start again. And keep going.

One of the things that Suzanne stresses strongly in all the well-being classes she facilitates is you have to know that it might take 100 times of something not working before the 101st try is a success. So don't stop yet. You don't know how many times something will take. But you do know it will take as many as it needs.

You start out with a try, and you have two options. You're either going to succeed or you fail. If you succeed, then you share it. From the share, you grow. From growing, you question. From questioning, you learn. And then you try again.

But if you try and you fail, then you learn and you try again. So failing actually gets you trying again quicker.

Chris got a really interesting perspective on this from the founder of a local company that owns a number of laundromats. He's grown his sons into the business. They're now in their mid to late 30s.

He said in the beginning, helping them to learn the business, he gave them a budget. He told them, "If the consequence of the failure is going to cost you $100 or more, come see me. Otherwise, handle it. Make the decision." He went on to say that after a while, that number became $500. He told them, "If the failure's going to cost $500, then come see me. Otherwise, make the decision and use it as a cost of education." Then it became $1,000, and then it went to $5,000, and ultimately it went to $10,000. He said, "So now, when you look at the consequences that they're able to deal with, there's nothing they're afraid to handle."

That's because he walked them through that from the beginning. What a blessing to be able to quantify the idea that, "It's okay. I know there's going to be a cost of education."

This example is a good way to look at respond versus react. The sons were able to respond with, "I know I have permission to handle this, so I'm going to handle it." That grew their ability to have less reaction, because reaction tends to not be thought out very well.

Let's wrap up the respond versus react discussion with a third "R" word: responsibility. There's a lot of talk about how everyone needs to take personal responsibility, which is a valid point. But here's an interesting way to look at the word responsibility. If you break it apart, you get these two words: response and ability. If you're taking responsibility, you're really developing your ability to personally respond. Your personal response ability is the key to being able to lead yourself well and handle your response to things. Then being proactive in your relationship space with your spouse and your children. It's communicating the vision well and working on the process so everyone understands their responsibility. What part of the load are they responsible for?

And then constantly reevaluating and asking, "How do we need to adjust all the weights on the plate so the plate doesn't fall over and break?" In other words, responding, not reacting.

TAKEAWAYS FROM THIS CHAPTER

A good business has processes in place in order to properly handle all situations. Shouldn't a family have the same? There's a big difference between responding and just reacting. Whether it's a set routine or having a structure in place, this helps parents to be a unified team when dealing with the kids, and helps spouses better deal with each other.

- Do you have family processes and standards?
- Understand that processes are dynamic and should be revisited and reassessed regularly.
- Do you have date nights? They can actually help your marriage in areas like communication and problem-solving.
- Failing is okay and an essential part of the process, but always try again.
- Responsibility = response and ability.

11

THE WISDOM OF WORDS

As you know, Suzanne has her own practice and Chris runs the family-owned auto dealerships. But every once in a while, we get the chance to work together. Chris brings Suzanne in to tap into her expertise, which helps in many ways. This chapter is the result of one of those times.

It started with a conversation about the next evolution of the business, as Chris' father continues to reduce his role and Chris and his sister continue to take greater roles. There were six of us at the table: the two of us, Chris' sister and her husband, and Chris' parents. Suzanne led a productive discussion about the shared wisdom of the six people in that room. Six people who have many things in common but who are all different, and who don't agree on everything but respect each other's opinion. That's important, because not every family or business leadership team can say that.

There can be a lot of wisdom in the words you say, but when you say a word, it doesn't mean others will go along with it. One does not imply the other. It's important to understand that there may be conflicts, but you can have good dialogues. Sometimes people hold their tongue because they don't want a conflict, but it's better to go ahead and have the discussion. When you avoid a subject, or there's an assumption of meanings, that can lead to a buildup of resentment. But when you realize not everybody understands your point of view, it can free you up quite a bit.

This all starts with these three statements, which Suzanne shared with the others:

- Acceptance does not equal agreement
- Understanding does not equal acceptance or agreement
- Opinion does not equal truth or fact

Let's unpack them individually. First, acceptance does not equal agreement. In today's society, many people seem to feel that if others don't agree with them, there's less value to that other person's thoughts. "You need to agree with me. Period, end of story." But we should be able to accept the fact that if someone doesn't see eye-to-eye with us, that doesn't make their thoughts less valuable. That doesn't make them less valuable as a person. When we stop assigning value to something, then we can just agree that it's going to be different for us.

You don't have to agree with someone's thoughts, opinions and values to accept them. They can be the complete opposite of yours, but you can still accept that person because they were made in the image of Christ, and you can't get any better than that. They have value simply because of being made in that image. That doesn't mean that I have to agree with you to accept that you're valuable. You can come into a situation and say, "We may not ever agree, but can't we accept one another for who we are?"

When you look at the three families represented in the room that day, we all attack things very differently. That comes from life experience, how we were raised, our family of origin. You can't expect to always have agreement from six different individual people. But we can accept that "You're my family, I love you, you have value, and maybe we just aren't going to be on the same path for this, but that's okay."

You need to know that there will be arguments, there will be conflict, but at the end of the day, we're family. We love one another and we have a common purpose, so let's figure out what's best for all parties. You may not get your way. But it might be you need time, and that's okay, as long as everyone understands that.

As a result of that conversation, all six of us are becoming more accepting, but we're asking more questions, and we're okay with that. It's freeing us up to do more of a deep dive into where our thoughts and processes come from. Not everyone will be right all the time. There is truth, and talking about opinion doesn't equal truth or fact. Agreeing on truth doesn't mean you're agreeing with someone's opinion. Everyone can be loving and accepting, but that doesn't mean we're always going to agree.

And why would you want that? That's actually the other key component of this. Would you want to have six people who have the exact same thoughts and opinions? Where are you going to go with that? If that's the case, there's nothing thought-provoking. There's nothing to encourage you to grow. There's a saying, "If you have a partner who agrees with you 100% of the time, one of you is useless."

We've talked a lot about how this relates to our family, but let's not forget, this started with a conversation about the business. There's good news on that front. Chris is beginning to see more people giving up this right to be right when they enter these discussions at work. Everyone has their own thoughts based on their life experiences. But if you go in thinking, "I could be wrong," or at least recognize there's another valid side of things, it can be really exciting to see how that conversation unfolds and what it can result in.

The second statement is understanding does not equal acceptance and/or agreement. This one stems from a discussion about what words we would use to describe our family, and where we felt we needed to do the most work. Someone said, "I think we could be more understanding." Suzanne interpreted that as meaning, "You could agree with me a little more and that would show your understanding." It's very common for people to believe that when they make a statement like this.

But a better way to look at understanding is to see it as compassion and caring. "I can have compassion for your situation and I can care deeply for you, but I don't have to accept your situation or agree that you're in a good situation." That doesn't negate or take away that area of understanding, which is compassion and care. I can still provide that for you and not have to be accepting of your thoughts or in agreement with them. Again, it goes back to valuing the individual person, simply because that person has value apart from how they may project or speak or have an opinion on different things.

What do you think would happen if people heard all three of these statements together? Maybe they would come to the conclusion, "There's some value there. I don't have to cancel somebody that I don't like. I don't have to unfollow someone that doesn't agree with me." Chris has spent a lot of time intentionally reading things he knew going in that he was going to disagree with. He knew it was an opinion very different from his own. That's helped him control his temper. It's given him a better understanding of where those opinions come from. He doesn't accept that point of view and he definitely doesn't agree with it, but he now has a level of understanding so if someone happens to express this particular belief and point of view, he can have a more thoughtful conversation.

We all come from different perspectives and life experiences. So if we choose to do so, we're able to take a step back and process how someone came to that thought or opinion or whatever you're discussing. How did they get there? Having an understanding of that background, giving some perspective on that, allows you to have a much more productive conversation. Even if you come from the opposite side, and you know how you see it and how you understand it, now you understand how they came to that. Again, you don't have to accept it or agree with it in order to be compassionate and kind in that moment.

Finally, opinion does not equal truth or fact. We touched on that a bit earlier. Again, everyone is different. The six people in that room had different families of origin, different life experiences through the formative years, different levels of education, and the list could go on. Our opinions are formed based on all of that. You may feel strongly about something, but that doesn't make it true. It doesn't create a fact in that situation. It's just how you feel. And you can't impose your strong feelings onto someone else and expect them to say, "You're exactly right, 100%. That is the gospel truth." No, it's just that you feel strongly about it. It's your opinion.

You may believe there are some black and white things that don't allow for opinion. But again, that's your opinion. No matter how strongly you hold an opinion, and how strongly the other person holds their opinion, it doesn't change the fact that these are opinions, not fact or truth. You don't have to agree, but you have to accept.

Here's an example from our church. There are essential doctrines in the Christian faith that we must all agree on 100%. You don't have to agree on the details of the day-to-day functioning of the church. You don't have to agree on who wears what, if it's acceptable to come in jeans and flip-flops or if you have to be dressed in a suit and tie. Those things don't matter. They're not an essential doctrine.

We should approach our life much in that same way. There are certainly essential things that we have to be in agreement on in order to function cohesively. But when we have differing opinions on things with someone else, neither of us can be so hard and fast on it that we see it as fact, because then we become arrogant and entitled.

This is where social media can be so problematic. Many people feel very comfortable expressing their opinion on social media, which leads to many others disagreeing with them online. It can get nasty. But they're just stating their opinion. If it rubs you the wrong way, you're certainly entitled to your own opinion, but don't respond to them thinking they need to agree with you.

A big part of today's cancel culture is the unwillingness or inability to decipher what is truth and fact. You need to dig. Over the last few years, there's probably not a single thing that's been in the news where you couldn't find "truth" on both sides.

You shouldn't be so married to your opinion that you deny truth or deny fact. You have to be willing to say, "Whoa, I read that wrong." On the flip side of that, if someone who has an opposing opinion to you that isn't based in truth or fact, and when they're faced with the facts they acknowledge that their opinion was wrong, you need to be accepting. "I get it. You were misled."

That's really where a lot of conflict comes from. There are so many opinions on social media and other online platforms that are conveyed as fact, and so many people just believe them. Have you heard of perpetuation? That's when a falsehood is told over and over again, until others take it as fact and truth.
In this chapter we've split out the business side of this and the family side. But for us, those sides are connected. With Chris in a family business, he is very aware of a troubling statistic. Less than 15% of family businesses survive to be passed down to the third generation. Chris and his sister are the second

generation leading the company, and the third generation is fast approaching adulthood.

We certainly don't want the business to disappear. Chris feels strongly that he needs to not just cultivate what his dad started, but steward it well and grow it so everyone involved has the ability to grow and flourish as well. So this conversation about acceptance and agreement and understanding and opinion and fact is very timely. If the family can rally around the three statements we've discussed and become unoffendable, the closeness of the family just keeps getting tighter, and that will bleed out into the business, because family and business are intertwined.

A big part of the understanding goes back to what you do at home. What you do as a family, and what you see as important. You'll have differences, but that's okay. As close as we all are, the three families in that room are different. We do different things. We approach things differently. We find enjoyment differently. But none of us believe one of the others has less value because of that.

It all boils down to valuing the other person. They have value simply because they exist. If you keep that value in your mind, that's going to temper how you approach different things. You know how something you say or do is going to be received. So you do that based on knowing "This person has value. I care about them. I'm going to be kind. We're different, but no less valuable."

So keep these three statements in mind:
- Acceptance does not equal agreement
- Understanding does not equal acceptance or agreement
- Opinion does not equal truth or fact

There's a lot of wisdom in these words.

TAKEAWAYS FROM THIS CHAPTER

What you say matters. How you say it matters. What you hear and how you receive those words can matter even more.

- Are you compromising your core values?
- Do you get offended when someone doesn't agree with you? Why do you think that is?
- How can you become a better listener to uncover what's being communicated?
- Do you agree with the three statements? Why or why not?

12

WHAT THE WORLD NEEDS NOW

We've talked about how our professional lives have intersected at times, particularly how Suzanne's experience and skills in coaching and counseling have been very helpful in the leadership development efforts at Chris' business.

As part of those efforts, they utilize an organization called Corporate Chaplains of America. They now have a chaplain to help employees and their families in their time of need, and also to talk confidentially with employees about things they may be struggling with. Chris gets a quarterly report on those issues at his business, along with nationwide data, and it's been an eye-opener.

The nationwide list directly reflects things Suzanne has discovered in his organization. Which means his employees are struggling with the same things as people nationwide. Many different types of people in many different types of businesses. It can be reassuring to know you're not alone in dealing with something.

The top three issues employees nationwide listed in their response to the survey are anxiety, depression, and stress management. Sound familiar to you? If you're an employer, chances are your employees are struggling with those same things…and you may be as well.

That list led us to this chapter. We want to talk about how to help people deal with those issues. When Suzanne works with people, whether individually or in group sessions, she talks a lot about controlling the controllables.

Bear in mind, there's a broad spectrum of anxiety and depression, so this is certainly not a one-size-fits-all answer, but in most cases, anxiety is from overthinking, from feeling overwhelmed. But a lot of the things being thought about, which are overwhelming them, are things they've created in their mind, not necessarily things that are concrete and tangible. Once you weed out the 99 out of 100 things that probably won't happen, you can say, "Okay, I can control this one thing," and you can focus on doing that. Then you look to the next thing and the next and the next, but it's more about using your voice, speaking what you need, speaking what you're feeling, and getting perspective on that. A lot of people who come and sit with her one-on-one will talk about anxiety and depression, and by the time they leave they say, "It was really nice to talk about that." Far too often, we hold everything so close to the chest that we don't allow ourselves to become open to other people, which means we have to carry it all.

There's a common saying in business: what isn't measured isn't managed. So, when you're feeling the overwhelming anxiety or the overwhelming depression, identify what things are happening that you can pinpoint to. If you can identify them, can you eliminate them? If so, you can take them out of your life. If not, how can you put them into a situation where you feel like you can manage them, and manage them well, so they're not going to end up being the rock around your neck?

When Chris works on leadership development with his team, they don't talk specifically about anxiety, depression, and stress management. They just narrow it down into two spaces, your mental space and your spiritual space, and which one do they want to work on? But usually when they dive into it, it's about experiencing some type of uncontrollable emotional response, which almost 100% of the time is an inability to handle stress.

Your brain can't tell the difference between an imagined fear and what's real. That's how we're wired to look at danger. Plus, having high chronic stress levels keeps our body in that fight-flight mode all the time. So, not only can our brain not discern, our body doesn't know what to do. Did we get a really hateful email, and we're automatically into that fight-flight spiral, or is there a tiger running towards us? Our body is having that same response because we haven't learned how to modulate that.

How does this play out for us? Anxiety, depression, and stress management all fall under mental health. How does this impact our physical health? What's the physical by-product of our mental state?

First, let's put stress at the top of the list. Not to minimize anxiety and depression, but a lot of times those two are exacerbated by uncontrolled stress. If you have uncontrolled stress in your life, not only does your body constantly stay in that adrenaline pumping mode, which is terrible on your nervous receptors, but you also typically have a higher resting heart rate, which means you don't get good sleep cycles, so your brain and body don't recharge. Your digestion is interrupted, so people suffer from things like irritable bowel syndrome. You may have heart palpitations. You may get tinnitus, that ringing in your ears. It just cascades. It's like a ripple. One thing happens, and if you don't have a good stress adaption, it just ripples out into everything. Then it flows into mood, which means you may bite the head off somebody who just looked at you the wrong way, or didn't hold the door long enough. Little things will make you snap.

There can also be a ripple effect in a positive way. A lot of the people who have completed the six months of leadership development have had this takeaway: "Man, this bled over into this and then it bled over into this, and then this." It always does. That's the whole idea of getting to an integrated life. Once you make the decision of who it is you're going to be, it bleeds over into everything. Then when you start doing things like learning how to handle stress management and depression, anxiety, again, it's not a one-size-fits-all, but it's a place to start.

We've talked in other chapters about how Chris uses cold exposure, whether that's standing barefoot in the snow or a cold shower or an ice bath. Doing that has helped him understand how his body reacts to stress, and get control of it. He's been advising people in his leadership development group to take cold showers, and a number of them have told him they can't believe how something that simple can affect the rest of their day. They don't get inflamed about things. They don't lash out. That's because taking that cold shower at the start of the day settles everything down and tells your body, "There are things I can control and things I can't," and recognizing the two.

It gives you perspective on how your body is going to respond to something because when you are uncomfortable, your body is telling you, "Get out, go. This is not good. You shouldn't be here." But when you stay in, and you realize, "Okay this sucked, but I made it," not only is that giving you a little control over your stress response, but it's also giving you the confidence to do hard things.

Far too frequently because we overthink, and we end up creating scenarios that typically don't happen, we don't allow ourselves the ability and the confidence to do hard things, handle them, and then go on to the next thing. We don't allow ourselves to get uncomfortable. How do you know what you're capable of if you're not allowing yourself to try those things?

Speaking of uncomfortable, when Chris tells his group to take a cold shower, he tells them to start by seeing if they could do 10 seconds. Once they do that, go a little longer and a little longer, with the ultimate goal of five minutes in an ice bath. Suzanne recommends doing it in the reverse. Get in with the water cold enough that you don't like it but not so cold that you want to jump back out, and stay in for 60 seconds. The next day, have the water a little colder. Keep doing that each day until it's as cold as possible. The idea is to not jump in feet first, just get it done.

You may have heard this statement: "If you can't make mistakes, then you can't make decisions." The fear of making mistakes keeps people from making a decision. Some stress comes from the inability to make a decision out of the fear of failure. Business leaders are often told, "Don't fail." Chris worked under that principle for a number of years, but then shifted to the concept of failing forward. There's a Japanese term called kaizen, which means change for the better, or continuous improvement. Kaizen is a business philosophy that concerns all processes that continuously improve operations, and involves all employees.

Toyota is a great example of kaizen, particularly in their production. They take an assembly line and get it going as fast as it possibly can, until it breaks. Then you go to where it broke and fix it, and turn it up, because now that's the new baseline.

Stress management can be the same way. You know what your baseline is, because that's where you're redlining. But if you can look at what's going on around that stress, and identify what's manageable, then you can control it and see where you're at after that. There's your new baseline. Because it's less about avoiding stress or the things that give you anxiety or depression, than it is about learning how to handle the things around them, and moving your baseline.

Too often, when people talk about anxiety, depression and the cycles that come with those things, they'll be managing well, making progress, they have momentum and they've got good traction, but then something happens and they're in the ditch. They forget all the good things they had put into practice and were working well for them. They go back to old habits and they get comfortable. Now they have to focus again on what was working well, and go back there. They're not starting over, it's more of a restart, but it's still hard work.

One of the important things we've learned is the importance of the ability to forgive yourself for failure and start over tomorrow. Tomorrow is always Day One. People have a tendence to say, "Monday begins a new week, so I'll start next Monday." If they fail on a Tuesday, once again, they wait till the following Monday, rather than saying, "Tomorrow is another day. I need to go again tomorrow." It's having that ability to self-forgive and understand what caused the failure, and start over right away. There are certainly times what caused the failure wasn't something you could control, but you can control how you react to it.

Sometimes that one simple little thing you might miss could be the one thing you need to do every single day for you to win every single day. If you're missing that one thing, that could be the lynch pin. And let's face it, winning is important. Even little wins. It's so beneficial to recognize when you're doing well. People don't do that often enough. But if you can intentionally put yourself in situations where you have to mark the wins, even the little ones, you're helping yourself in a big way.

You have to celebrate what you got right. Suzanne no longer asks people how they're doing. Now, when she sees someone that she hasn't seen in a while, whether that's a client or a friend, she asks them, "Hey, what's new and good?" She wants people to focus on what's propelling them forward, because the bad stuff, the unhappiness, the unsettledness, are all temporary. You could be better in 10 minutes.

You may be wondering what all this has to do with the faith aspect of this book. Stress and faith really go hand in hand. It's not just recognizing that there are things you can control. If we also recognize that there is someone in control, it helps to develop the faith muscle of, "I know there's a sovereign plan and it's going to be okay." Developing that muscle can be a daunting task.

That's a pretty big missing piece of the puzzle a lot of times. Some people say there are pillars in our lives. Suzanne likes to call them primary foods, and spirituality is a very important one. If you're not connected to something bigger than you, then you feel like you have to carry everything, and you can't do that. We're not built to do that. That's not how we're made.

Sometimes when she has a client like that, she'll say, "The world must be very heavy for you. You're carrying all these different things around every single day. What can you offload?" When the client says they can't offload certain things, the question becomes, "Okay, now what are you going to do with those? Who are you going to give them to because they're not yours to carry, so where are they going to go?" Which does lead to a lot of faith conversations.

That also happens in the leadership development program at Chris' business. When people complete the work, they often say they can't believe how much one aspect bleeds into another. They work on calibration, which is mental and spiritual. They work on their physical well-being, how they show up conditionally. They work on relationships. They work on how they show up in their community. How do they show up for their family, their job, or their church? Sometimes those relationships show up in their community. And it all flows into their mental space.

Much of the stress people deal with is financial. There's a lack of finances to do what they want, or even what they need. That may start at work, but it definitely flows into the home, into the family. But if you can learn how to show up as an example of how to handle stress well, that also can bleed over into the family. How the family performs as a unit, and how you and your spouse form the relationship and handle things together. Learning what you have to do to manage the stress, so you show up differently than you were before. This could lead to the spouse observing the same thing and going about the same processes. The whole family unit is going to benefit from just one person learning how to manage stress.

This leads into fulfillment in every space. It's not about doing everything perfectly. It's about doing it a little bit better than yesterday. If you're showing up a little better than you did yesterday, you're doing a little more work than you did yesterday. You're staying uncomfortable a little longer than you did yesterday. You're making one better decision today than you did yesterday. All these things multiply over time. They compound and grow into really big things.

It's the power of one more. That's actually the title of a great book by Ed Mylett. It speaks directly to how are you developing more than you were yesterday? One more, then another, and another after that. It bleeds into every aspect.

So let's wrap up with some final thoughts on making those aspects of your life better, and more positive. The advice Suzanne gives to her clients is relevant to anyone struggling with stress.

It's so important to get really clear on what you want, what you need, and what you value. Because a lot of times what we think we need is actually a want that's showing up because we have this hole that we don't know how to fill. If you can get really clear on your wants, needs and values, then you can get really clear on where you need to place some energy and really pour into one or more spaces.

And talk to somebody. It doesn't have to be someone who's credentialed. Just get it out. If you don't, things can ping pong in your brain to the point where you're no good to anyone. You also have a great tool in your hand. Our phones are amazing devices for verbal vomit. Just record the message. Don't just let the thought sit and stew, because the longer you do that, the more things you'll think of that probably won't ever happen.

You're going to think about the negative. Remember, thoughts turn into things. If your thinking is not in a good place, it's going to create things that are not in a good place. If you're in a negative mindset, you're only going to see the negative. If you look for enough problems, you will find plenty. Whereas if you're looking for things that are good, that are positive, that are encouraging and edifying, you're going to find those too, and you're going to bring more of that. But whichever way you go, you're going to have to do some hard evaluating, and it's never good to do that by yourself.

TAKEAWAYS FROM THIS CHAPTER

If you're dealing with anxiety, depression, or stress management, you're far from alone. Those are the most common issues facing employees nationwide. But they don't have to overwhelm you. By determining what you can control, you can focus on one thing at a time, manage it, and then move on. If it's something you can't control, don't let it take control of you.

- What do you want, need, and value?
- How do you control the controllable - do you even know what they are?
- Do you have a trusted friend, colleague or professional to whom you can unload your stress?
- Are you stuck in fight/flight/freeze? What's keeping you stuck? How can you break your cycle?
- How do you remind yourself to lean into faith and God's plan when things are hard?

WHAT'S NEXT?

Since we began this book with a couple questions, it seems fitting that we end it the same way.

Let's start with the one at the top of this page. What's next for you, now that you've read this book? What are the next steps on your journey? What will you do with the information and insights we've shared?

As we said back at the beginning of the book, we hope you'll use it as a conversation starter. Because open and honest communication is the key to a successful relationship... whether that's with your spouse, your kids, your employees or coworkers, or any other relationship that's important to you.

Sometimes those conversations can be difficult. Sometimes you each see things differently. Which is okay. No matter how much you love each other, you're not going to agree on everything. But hopefully you'll agree on this: avoiding the conversation is worse than having it. Because if you respect each other, which is one of the foundations of a successful relationships, a frank and open conversation can open your eyes to what's truly possible.

We've talked about our own difficult conversations in this book. We've also shared a lot about ourselves. Perhaps there were times that made you a little uncomfortable. That certainly wasn't our intention. We didn't do it to just say, "Hey, look at us." We did it to say, "Hey, look at what we've been through. Look at what we've learned from this. Can this help you deal with what you're going through?"

In fact, there may have been times while reading this book that you said, "Wow, they could be talking about us." Too often, when we go through something, we feel alone. We think we're the first ones to deal with this situation.

But that couldn't be further from the truth. We're never alone. There's always someone to talk to. Sometimes that's a professional, like Suzanne. Sometimes that's a member of the clergy, or someone else from your church. Or sometimes it's a private conversation with God. Because your faith can help you get through the tough times. It's done that for us numerous times. Our faith has also helped to make the good times even better. Faith can be the foundation for a better relationship and a better life.

So, let's go back to the question we're using the wrap up this book. What's next? What are your next steps? More important, what's your first step?

Hopefully your first step is to have that first conversation. To help you get started, we asked you a few questions at the end of each chapter. Have you answered them yet? Have you and your spouse talked about them?

We're happy to be part of your conversations. The QR code on the next page will take you to our website. It contains the latest information about us, including Suzanne's ministry and Chris' coaching. It also has a link to our podcast, where we continue to share experiences and insights similar to the ones in this book. It also gives you ways to contact us.

We don't have all the answers. But sometimes just asking the right questions, whether that's of someone else or yourself, can steer you in the right direction. We hope this book will help you make your journey a good one!

READY TO START THE CONVERSATION?
Open your eyes to what's *truly* possible.

To Learn More
About Us and the
**Faith. Family. Fulfillment
Community,** go to:

FaithFamilyFulfillmentPodcast.com

or, scan the QR code!

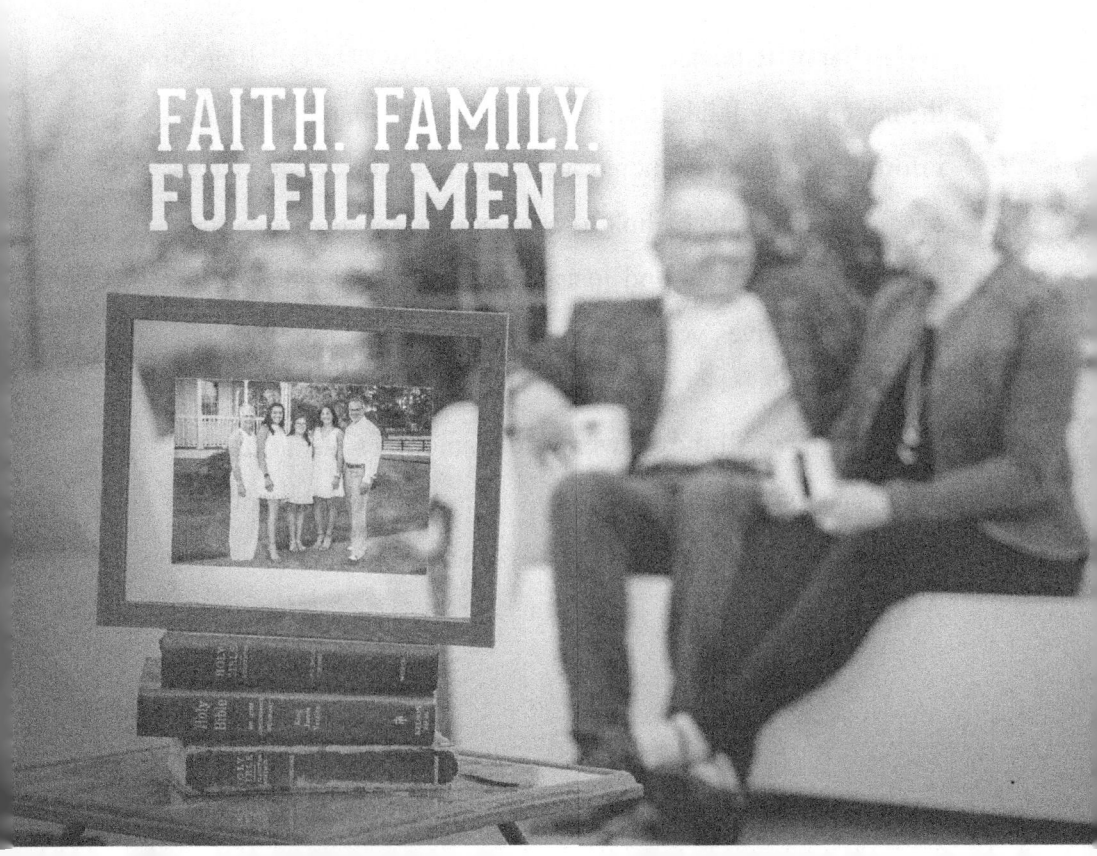

FAITH. FAMILY. FULFILLMENT.

Be sure to check out our first book in the

FAITH. FAMILY. FULFILLMENT.
— Series —

Listen to Our Podcast

New Episodes Air Thursday

On *Faith. Family. Fulfillment.* Chris and Suzanne Vester discuss the topics of creating a strong bond and having a loving relationship through Christian values. Each week, listeners can tune in to hear stories and discussions from guests, ranging from faith pastors and family counselors, to people just like you, describing the importance of staying the course and providing wisdom and lifelong lessons to one another. Chris and Suzanne invite you to strengthen your core and create a trusting and loving bond on Faith, Family, and Fulfillment. https://apple.co/34aGj3h

WANT TO PUBLISH A BOOK LIKE THIS?

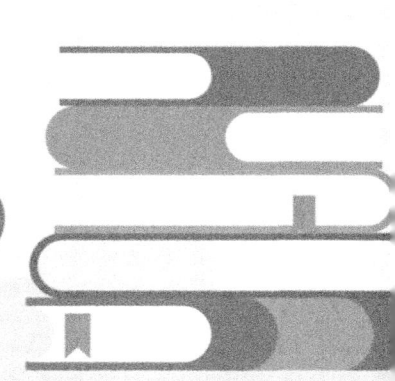

BMD PUBLISHING HAS PUBLISHED DOZENS OF BOOKS LIKE THIS IN NUMEROUS BUSINESS SECTORS.

OUR PROCESS IS EFFICIENT AND EFFECTIVE.

IF YOU'VE ALWAYS WANTED TO DO A BOOK BUT DIDN'T KNOW WHERE TO BEGIN, GO TO WWW.MARKETDOMINATIONLLC.COM/BMDPUBLISHING TO SET UP A FREE *TURN THE PAGE* CONSULTATION.

BEGIN AN EXCITING NEW CHAPTER IN YOUR LIFE!

IT'S YOUR TIME TO BECOME AN AUTHOR